DECENT PASSIONS

MICHAEL DENNENY

DECENT PASSIONS

Real Stories about Love

Boston • Alyson Publications, Inc.

To My Mother and Father

And for Jay

Also by Michael Denneny

Lovers: The Story of Two Men

The Christopher Street Reader
(edited with Charles Ortleb and Tom Steele)

A paperback original from Alyson Publications, Inc., PO Box 2783,
Boston, Massachusetts 02208. Typeset and printed in the U.S.A.

First edition, first printing: March 1984

ISBN 0 932870 39 2

CONTENTS

11 Introduction: Real Stories

17 The Studio 54 Clown and the Street Queen
19 Robert
49 Timmy

81 The Liberated Don Juan and the Cypriot Beauty
83 Mark
118 Danae

149 The Viking on the Battlements and the Chicken Soup Lady
151 Beth
190 Sally

219 Afterword: Passion and Decency

ACKNOWLEDGMENTS

I would like to thank all the people with whom I talked in the course of this project, especially the couples whom I interviewed. The reader will get some sense of the integrity, generosity, and friendliness of the people presented here; only I know and appreciate the same qualities in those people who, for one reason or another, were not included in the book. I am grateful to all those who shared their lives with me.

I would like to thank Jane Rotrosen, whose elan and belief in this project (and in me) really carried it off and whose acute editorial comments made her much more than an agent to me; Chuck Ortleb, who never seems to get tired of talking with me, no matter how obsessive I am; Paul Dinas at St. Martin's Press, who almost kept my office and life in order while I was doing this project; and John Preston, who has contributed to this book in so many ways he's in the amusing position of being its midwife.

Finally I would like to thank Sasha Alyson. If he had not had the initiative and energy to create an excellent gay publishing house, this book would never have seen the light of day.

But such reaching out in passion does not simply lift us up and away beyond ourselves. It gathers our essential being to its proper ground, it exposes our ground for the first time in so gathering, so that the passion is that through which and in which we take hold of ourselves and achieve lucid mastery over the beings around us and within us.

—Martin Heidegger

INTRODUCTION
Real Stories

When I embarked on this project, I had reached what seemed like a state of terminal confusion. For some years I had felt most truly alive when I was in love. Although I was intensely involved in my work, enjoyed a group of wonderful friends, and took advantage of the excitement a big city can offer, none of these things by themselves — or even together — seemed to constitute a happy life. If my love life was desolate, everything seemed out of whack. Romance and passion supplied a vitality and happiness nothing else quite matched; without love, life seemed not only barren but pointless. I think I assumed that love *was* the point of life. This can get you in trouble. I not only piled up the usual quota of hard knocks and halcyon days, blissful nights and bitter mornings, I gradually became more and more confused about what I was doing. It was clear I wasn't getting what I wanted; but then again, what precisely did I want? And was it even possible? Or was I only suffering the aftereffects of a fading adolescent fantasy?

Thinking about the situation didn't help much. Introspection only muddled me more and talking about it exhaustively to my friends only exhausted them and me. Love seemed to me so confusing, difficult, and ultimately demoralizing that I wasn't sure I wanted it — but without it my life felt somehow empty. For a while I considered the possibility that I was a bit demented about the whole subject, had become a monomaniac or fallen victim to the romantic hype of the media, with its endless stories and songs about love and passion. But as I looked around me it seemed clear enough that love *was* the most important thing in life for most people. It seemed to offer a dramatic intensity and a happiness — from exuberance to ecstasy to deep satisfaction — that most of us can't find anywhere else. Who hasn't felt the astonishment that comes with the first touch of love when everything seems possible again? When the world opens and you feel like you've woken up? The kiss that released Sleeping Beauty, the recognition that allowed the toad to become the prince he truly is — that incredible feeling of passion, which sometimes survives but more often doesn't, is an experience felt by virtually everyone at some moment in their lives.

But who hasn't become entangled in the misery it can cause? The snares of jealousy and fear of not being loved as much as one loves. The pain of not being wanted sexually when one wants to be wanted sexually. The grating discrepancies in daily habits and outlook that seem so trivial at first but can build up until they affect you like chalk screeching on a blackboard. The furious frustration of not being understood. The dilemmas of personal freedom versus commitment and responsibility. For me, the utter demoralization of losing a lover undercut my sense of self so much I began to wonder if the risk and the grief were worth it, and whether it was ever possible to make things work.

In this state of confusion, I decided I wanted to hear how other people handled these matters, to see if their stories could shed any light on my own dilemmas. It seemed there were endless experts telling me how to do everything, from making love and having sex to building a relationship or at least learning how to make friends with myself. But while these books often have a lot of simple common sense mixed in with the oversimplified nonsense and hype necessary to attract attention, they only work as temporary morale boosters, Sunday sermons that uplift us for an hour and have no impact on how we actually live our lives — or at least how I actually live my life. I wanted to talk to real people who had experienced passion and thought about it, the way we all think about things that matter to us, people who could communicate their experience in its actual weight and density. There are no experts in love as there are no experts in life. We're all in the same boat, and sharing our experience — hard-won as all lived experience is — seemed a sensible idea.

So I went out and talked to many couples, some at length. These people were remarkably open and generous in sharing their lives, as anxious as I to understand what had happened to them, while clarifying for themselves what they had and what they wanted. I made no effort to interpret or analyze what I heard, which may irritate adherents of various schools of psychology or sociology. Frankly I am dubious about any attempt to penetrate and explain the recesses of the human heart. Anyway, it would have been beside the point. These were stories and I was a listener. I tried not to bring prefabricated *explanations* to what I heard, but to follow the speaker and let the story emerge as it wanted. This led to some surprises: matters I would have thought significant did not emerge on their own, and other themes that I had not considered emerged strongly. The point was not to interpret but *to listen*. You do not necessarily understand a good story the first time you hear it, and your understanding of it may change over time.

It is important that these are real stories; they happened to particular people. There is no attempt here to commit a social science. The six individuals in this book are *not* a representative sample, or a composite portrait, or anything else. They are real people and like all real people they are unique. Their stories are completely individual and particular — which seems fitting. Whether or not there is such a thing as a representative portrait — the average, the norm, the general — you certainly don't find it in love affairs. Love seems to be precisely about the discovery and celebration of the *particular* person, "who" we are as opposed to "what" we might be in the world.

Real stories are always unlikely. And love, as common as it is, is the unlikeliest thing of all. By some odd psychological trick — or perhaps it's just mental laziness, a numbness induced by the watered-down social science vision of life the media saturates our world with — we increasingly tend to see ourselves as exemplifying various generalities. We nod our heads as we are told in countless books, magazines, and talk shows that we are alienated from a dehumanized social system, suffering from the frantic narcissism of the me generation, fleeing intimacy and fighting responsibility, or suffering the shock of a breakdown of values.

But even if true, what in the world do you *do* with this knowledge? This type of thinking leads us to being spectators at our own lives — and inattentive spectators at that. Made drowsy by a surfeit of artificial images of what life is like, we fail to see the reckless improbability of the real thing. Strangeness — peculiarity, singularity — is the hallmark of reality. All we have to do is reflect for a moment on the story of our own concrete lives to realize how odd it is. Everybody has a story and everybody's story is passingly strange. I have found that *whenever* I set out to interview anyone and really concentrated my attention on them, they would be transformed into something "rich and strange" before my eyes. To trade the strangeness of reality — the magic of life — for a likely story that has been processed through the strainer of some grid of interpretation, seems to me a poor bargain. I tend to believe that it is the virtue of stories that in them the particular, in its very particularity, can reveal some truths that otherwise could not be grasped. In any event, I have found that some stories have a clarity which is illuminating. This illumination works in obscure ways that I certainly haven't figured out, but I suspect it is the secret of the value fiction has for us.

But these stories are real, not fiction. The following interviews reveal one moment in the lives of the people interviewed. All these love affairs were ongoing; what happened the next day, the next week, the next year would, of course, change the story and how the teller told it. That would always be the case, at any point in time. To supply an ending — how did it turn out, did they live happily ever after? — would be precisely to turn these real stories into fiction. Fiction is finished, life isn't. And life doesn't finally make sense the way fiction does, because fiction is one way we make sense of life.

I did not want to force my way of making sense onto these people. My aim is to make sense of my own life; listening to how other people make sense of theirs seems useful. The book that has resulted consists of six interviews that tell the story of three love affairs. Little of significance has been altered and only incidental matters have been omitted. I have, of course, edited them; what you will read is only a fraction of the transcripts of the interviews. I have tried to retain the surface texture of spoken speech and follow the rhythm of the stories as they unfolded, with the hesitations and reflective pauses and the sudden onrush of certainty. I sought diversity in age, station in life, geography, sexual orientation, etc. — not to construct a representative portrait of love and passion today, but simply to get three *different* stories.

An interview, unlike a fictional story, captures one moment in an ongoing life; thus what comes into focus is what people are striving for, what they affirm in their lives and what they want. The essential question is one of values — what do I want, what can I hope for, what should I accept. I have found these conversations to be of immense value for myself, especially in clarifying the importance of common decency and the startling idea that it can and ought to be combined with our most intense passion. To talk to people about the ultimate and concrete values in their life always seems to me useful. I hope it proves useful — illuminating, provocative, confirming — to the reader and can serve as a stimulus to the efforts of each of us to make sense of our own lives.

Robert & Timmy

The
Studio 54 Clown
and the
Street Queen

I met Robert and Timmy in their small, two-and-a-half room apartment in Manhattan, on the lower Upper West Side, a couple of blocks from Lincoln Center. Their severely limited space has been excellently designed for living; it is stylish, comfortable, and functional. Shades of gray and off-white combine with unexpected pastels and natural wood in a simple up-to-date industrial aesthetic with flashes of whimsy. Robert is compactly and elegantly put together, a well-built body, open, boyish face, short hair, T-shirt and jeans. He is twenty-two, an aspiring interior designer working as a salesclerk until his freelance business is more solidly established. Timmy wears a loose football jersey, jeans, sneakers, a crooked smile and a quizzical expression on an Irish face under black curly hair; at twenty-four he's held a variety of odd jobs and just finished collaborating on a successful screenplay. Both radiate a youthful bodily energy that can make one feel old and wry at the same time.

ROBERT

Tell me how you met Timmy.

Well, I had been seeing a guy named Johnnie, a hot little Puerto Rican. All along Johnnie was on and off with his lover, but Johnnie was very much into sex. I was new in New York and I just enjoyed having sex with him. One night we had a date to go to the movies, and I went all the way up to Seventy-ninth Street, and everybody was getting ready to go out (laughs) — Johnnie, his lover, and another couple... and he just said to me, "I'm going out." There's one thing about Johnnie: he has *no* tact. I kind of hid everything but I felt so stupid that this asshole was going somewhere with his lover and he didn't even call me up and cancel. I was really pissed.

Anyway, I had been hanging out at the Stud in the Village, so I went down there. I trashed around a little bit and was on my way out, because I had just had it. And I turned around — if you ever go to these trash bars, you look around and see if there's anything you like, you know, you cruise around and check it out. And in the middle of the room there's a post — it kind of reminds me of a cowboy post in a corral. And he was right near there. He had on baggy pants and he seemed very thin and he had short curly hair, close-cropped, and a baggy white shirt. He looked, interestingly enough, like a Puerto Rican to me, this nice little Irish boy. (Laughs) So I went over to him and, uh... I thought he was hot... I thought I could get into this. So I just like grabbed his crotch or something, and he responded. And that's the sign — you take it from there. So we had a hot little session against the wall — I can still flash back to it very vividly, the session against the wall. Umm, and we ended it and went over to the bar, and I think I got a beer. He said something like, "Boy, that was hot," and I said, "Yeah." And he was going to take the subway uptown, so I walked him to the subway. Then I got real brave and said, "I really would like to fuck with you." I think at that time it meant getting fucked, rather than fucking. And he said, "Yeah, I'd like that too." But he was really discouraging me from going home with him because of where he lived. He said it was really a mess and "I got dogs" — something to that effect. I said, "I really don't care." I just kept telling him, "I really don't care. I just want to spend the night." So we took the subway.

I was immediately fascinated by him because he seemed very cynical about a lot of things. He was more than just a body at that point, that evening — I realized this guy was... very interesting. And I really wasn't sure how old he was.

Do you normally go out with people your own age?

Yeah. Though I had this one little fling, and he was around forty, but he had also modeled and he was very handsome and dressed very stylishly, which at that time meant something, but not anymore. (Laughs)

So we got off the subway and I didn't really know that much about New York, but this didn't look like a particularly nice neighborhood.

You'd been living in New York...?

Three months. I was living in Brooklyn Heights, which is very, very nice as far as New York neighborhoods go. And before that I was living in white, middle America in Philadelphia, so I really wasn't prepared for that poverty and I was very uneasy walking down Fiftieth Street in that neighborhood....

Hell's Kitchen?

But he described it as — and we still talk about it to this day as — "not quite north of Hell's Kitchen." Something like that: not quite north of Hell's Kitchen. It was little things — when he talked like that —that I picked up on, that said this guy is special.

What was your first reaction to the apartment?

Well. (Laughs) I couldn't believe it — you know we were walking up four flights of these very rickety stairs in this sleazy, dirty, fluorescent-lighted stairwell. I was talking on the way up, and he kept saying, "Quiet, I've got dogs, and they're gonna start barking, and I live with this girl." And I didn't know what to think of that. As a matter of fact I think I asked, "Is she a lesbian?" And he said "I don't really know." (Laughs) I don't think we even know to this day what her situation is. But when I got into the apartment, it was — I was kind of freaked when I got into the apartment and saw the poverty... and the bathroom. You know, roaches and all that. It was very much unlike anything I had ever seen. And there was no light in the bathroom — (laughs) there was only a candle in there. It was a railroad flat, but you could look out one window in the kitchen and see the Empire State Building. That was something he pointed out right away, and I was like, wow, somebody I know has a view of the Empire State Building! So that was interesting. But it was very depressing. I felt uncomfortable. There were roaches everywhere — and there were tons of dogs, I just saw dogs and cats for days — animals everywhere.

How many?

I think three dogs and six cats — three dogs and five cats — Raoul hadn't come yet. I just didn't know what to think of these people who had all these animals... I didn't understand, you know? The dogs were barking a lot, and then Patti came in and I met her, and she seemed sweet. And us, we went upstairs — we went up to the roof. It was beautiful up there. That was a mystical experience — the roof. It was one of those cool summer evenings, and from the roof you have a *wonderful* view of the Empire State Building lit up. It was fabulous. And the Bell Telephone building was beautiful during the summer night. Looking around the city was very — we had gotten high, I think, on the way home, so it was an extraordinary experience. Then Patti came up with the dogs and the dogs shit, because they had a little penned area, and Patti went downstairs at a certain point and we just carried on.

You made love on the roof?

Yeah. And that was fabulous. It was cool, breezes flying... and I didn't feel at all uncomfortable that it was a roof — I felt very safe up there. For a long time I felt safe on the roof at night, in the evenings; it was just a wonderful feeling.

Did the sex go well?

Yes. I don't remember that much about it, except at some point being fucked by Timmy and he got into it and he was fucking me hard, and I didn't particularly like it. But then again, I never did like to get fucked, because it hurt too much, and I didn't do it that much. But everybody said, "Ooh, such a nice ass, I want to fuck it" (laughs), so I was constantly plagued by people just wanting to fuck my ass. But Timmy wasn't really that way at all. He seemed to care about what I wanted, and I wanted to please him too. So sexually it got off very well.

What happened the next morning?

Oh, I don't remember. But I liked him. Period. And I decided to call him again at some point, which I did. We always write our numbers on little pieces of paper, but this time I decided I would actually call him.

What was your background? You had been in New York three months. Where had you lived before that?

Philadelphia, white middle-class America. You were afraid of Negroes, you didn't know Jews, and you made fun of them. You went to high school and you really didn't go to college but you got a girlfriend and at some point got a car and then got married and lived in the neighborhood. And if you aspired to anything different than that — well, you were really looked down upon. It was very, very safe there. You could leave any doors open at night. It was suburban, just a very neat little place. And that was one thing I always found difficult in New York and still do, all the trash, the filth — just the untidiness of it all. But Brooklyn Heights was interesting, and I really started getting into it when I looked around at other neighborhoods and saw how people were living. I felt as safe there as I could in New York City.

I had gone to architecture school in the middle of the Pennsylvania countryside, as rural as you could get. I had only been away from that a year and I had enjoyed that very much. So I had very definite feelings about how I wanted to live. And definite feelings about how people should live. And that's what turned me off immediately to Timmy's environment. I couldn't see how someone could live like this, and I really felt sorry for him for a long time. And I didn't really even want to be in that apartment . . . .

Why did you move to New York?

Why did I move to New York? Uh . . . because there was no chance of me getting anywhere or being anything in Philadelphia. I wanted to be a designer and I knew New York was the place for it. And a person I was friends with in college moved here the year that I graduated.

He wrote me how wonderful New York was and all the things he was doing. Meanwhile I was back home, just existing. My parents had found out that I was gay, and living at home was really horrible. It was a horrible experience. I had a job working for a designer, but I didn't really see myself going anywhere. And my friend Jerry just seemed to get these opportunities to do things and experience things that I wasn't experiencing, and he gradually, over a period of about nine months, told me that I'd have to come to New York. And I visited him periodically, like every two months. And I fell in love with the freedom *immediately*. The gay freedom. Christopher Street was amazing to me the first time. Seeing that. And the pace was fabulous. I enjoyed the pace, the people, the traffic. I was afraid of crime and everything, but once I got here and saw that people weren't stabbing each other in the streets, and I had only positive experiences, I decided to give it a try. From college we had a mutual friend who was living in Brooklyn Heights and his having to leave New York coincided exactly with my moving up. I came up about a month before to start looking for work and went into Conran's on Third Avenue and got a job there.

What kind of job?

A salesman, a salesperson. Con's is like The Workbench. Everything from furniture to dishwear to fabrics and all that stuff. I was just a salesperson, but the salary was okay. I was absolutely thrilled to be on my own. I got the job about a month before coming. Then I found out about this apartment, and I took care of all that with Jerry.

Your roommate?

(Laughs) Jerry. Yes. Well, she was such a queen. After I broke off friendship with Jerry, I asked myself: why the fuck did I ever want to bother with this guy. But I know why. I mean we had design in common, we had fashion in common, we had upward mobility in common, and of course, he moved to New York and turned me on to it. So....

Were you lovers, or just—

Oh no! God no!

Just friends?

No. Just friends.

Okay, I just wanted to know.

Well, I'd like to dish him, but he really did play an important part in my life in getting me up here. And that I will always be thankful for.

So getting back to the first time you called Timmy. You called him?

Yes. Neither one of us I think remembers what we decided to do after that first meeting. It was just... to go over his place or go to a movie or whatever.

One of the earliest things I remember is that he took me to a movie screening where I went ga-ga. I mean, here I was in the same room with Jack Nicholson, Diana Ross. God, there were models galore... Ummm, Warren Beauty. Liv. Fucking Liv Ullman, who didn't like my boots. (Laughs) I had just gotten a pair of cowboy boots. I mean, I saved — I didn't even eat — for these boots. I was very fashion conscious at the time. (Laughs) So these boots were about $120, and I had no savings, but I figured, fuck it, I'm going to spend the money for these boots. And Liv Ullman didn't like them.

Timmy got invited through work?

Through Ray. But that was one of the few times we went to something like that. Timmy was right about that scene. And I feel kind of silly about my reactions at the time, but I guess that was the way I felt. But look, he was pretty jaded by then, you know, he'd had millions of years more experience in gay life than I did.

You were how old at this time?

Ummm... twenty-two.

And Timmy was?

Twenty-three I guess.

You thought him cynical?

Yeah, and I told him that. And he said... "You know, you're wrong about the cynicism," and then I don't remember how he explained it. As being something else. But, let's face it, I was very, very positive when I first came to New York. I was hyped up for my job at Conran's, even though it was a lowly sales job. And he just seemed... I remember him saying things about the Catholic Church. And back then I was going to church. You know, sarcastic comments about nuns and priests and stuff like that. And I figured, well this guy really doesn't have a very good opinion about very many things.

Then there was a period of dating?

Yeah. Dating. And sex.

How often were you seeing one another?

I guess once a week.

And what do you remember about that period?

Ah... the sex. (Laughs) I guess, yeah, okay. I remember... a twin-sized bed, against the wall in a corner of the room, he had a blue light in his room at the time. Very, very small room. And it was very uncomfortable seeing roaches on the walls, and *tons* of cat hair, cause the cats were allowed to roam the apartment free. *Tons* of cat hair. And my allergy was really bad. We could always predict when I was going to start sneezing. We could almost look at a watch and say go, and I would start sneezing. They would always have some sort of allergy pills that they would give me which would make me sleepy. By day, Timmy always was around. We would smoke dope and get real high. It did seem like a very loving place. When you came in, the dogs jumped all over you, and it was just a very warm feeling. But it was uncomfortable because of the poverty. We always used to have ice cream or something like that. One of the things he made me, which I loved, was an English muffin with butter and cinnamon on it. We got into making those all the time. So I had really nice feelings about going over there, you know, and going to bed with this blue light on and having sex. And waking up the next morning and not wanting to leave, but leaving. During this time I left Conran's and went to work at the Storehouse on Christopher Street. And that was another trip for me — working on Christopher Street. But I saw it again as a step up in my life — I was interested in stepping up at the time.

Were your feelings in this period mainly sexual?

Yeah. And, as I said, I perceived that he was a very special person . . . but very cynical. He made me feel uncomfortable about what he was attacking and how he attacked it. And he seemed jaded. But I was still fascinated. And I was a little bit — I was *a lot* frightened by his intelligence. 'Cause Timmy . . . is what I simply classify as a *deep thinker*. And he really has good touch with his feelings. I went through my whole life just accepting this or accepting that, or getting hurt by this, but not really thinking very much. I never figured I had to think about a lot of these emotional things since my emotional experiences were never very deep. And if they were, I really didn't know how to handle them. So I really seemed lightweight. Like on my birthday. . . .

What happened?

Um, well, of course we had made plans to spend my birthday at Studio 54 and, ah, at the time I was into angel dust (laughs) cause the guy I was working with was turning me on to it. Michel was a very

Village-type person, into all these heavy things, and angel dust was one of them. So he gave me a joint of dust for my birthday, and I decided with Jerry and another friend that we were going to spend my birthday at Studio and do dust, and just really freak out. And I knew that night there was going to be some kind of political rally because the bill had just been defeated, about discrimination against gays — and Tim was going to march. I was working at the store until eight and Timmy had said he was going to stop by at some point, but in the meantime my friend Alan came by. Alan was an airline steward who drank nothing but champagne. So he brought champagne down, and we were drinking champagne and I think smoking a little dust. Then Timmy walks in, and I had just come from downstairs in the storeroom for some reason, to get something... or to lock up because it was getting close to eight.... So I had to check some doors downstairs and I must have been hanging all over him when Timmy walked in (laughs) — Timmy had these presents for me, and (laughs) I mean, looking back I really feel horrible because I... it looked... I mean, my shirt was off, Alan's shirt was off, but we weren't... Well, I *had* tricked with Alan. He bought a chair and he asked me if we delivered — because he lived upstairs, in the apartment building above the store — and he asked me if we deliver, and, uh, I said sure.... So I went up and delivered (laughs)... I think I only tricked with him once, but I like him, and we had gotten into going to Studio together. And Timmy walked in, and he had this card with all the animals footprints all over.... (Laughs)

He had all the animals sign the card?

It was just so sweet, you know, I really felt wonderful when he gave me the card. But on the other hand I was dusted and drunk, so I was really spaced out, and then he gave me these two books. I must have just thumbed through them very stupidly, but I never realized that he was so — so upset over it.

So then he went off to a political rally and you went off to Studio 54?

Yeah... yeah. I could tell he was very uncomfortable and I tried to make him feel comfortable, but it wasn't working. He said he had to go, but he had this wonderful, sweet expression on his face and this smile — kind of embarrassed about the whole thing. I really didn't realize he was that upset because I thought he would sense that I was on something. As a matter of fact I said I'm really wasted, I'm on dust and everything, you'll have to excuse me, or something like that. But I guess I really made him feel bad.

Did you go out dancing with Timmy a lot?

No, no. That was always a sore spot because Mr. Snob would not go out dancing. It seemed to me at the time that he was above it all. And we weren't that close. I didn't prove myself to be very competent in handling any kind of emotional conversation, so he didn't really get to tell me about how he felt, about why he didn't go out. So I just figured this was somebody that's young, and yet he's not into any of these things, and I can't imagine why.

Did you find a big difference between your styles?

Yeah! (Laughs) Yeah, that was a big problem.

How did it manifest itself?

Well, I didn't like the way he dressed. Period. I was a real snob about that. And I perceived he didn't like the way I dressed either. We didn't even have to talk about it — it was very obvious that we didn't like the way each other dressed. (Laughs)

Did it lead to any conflicts?

No. Except — I mean he told me I looked *great* on Valentine's Day, but from what he said the other day I could see that he must have thought I was an asshole or something because I had on a red top — very, um, Hemingway lipstick top. Johnnie Martinez was designing really far-out things for me and he was just getting carried away. I was a Studio clown — you know, one of those people who got dressed up for Studio and carried on. It's hard for me to admit that now because it seems such a stupid thing to do . . . so immature . . . but I did it anyway. (Laughs)

Were you sleeping with other people?

Yeah, tricks. Probably only once a week — a Friday or Saturday night kind of thing because I was working Monday through Friday and Sunday. And I was working on my apartment for a while too, so that was taking up a lot of my evenings. Around Christmas I had an affair with that older model type. He came into the store and bought something and liked me, and we got together.

When did your feelings toward Timmy start developing beyond sexual attraction and interest?

Ummm... I guess somewhere in the period before Christmas. I began to feel like I wanted to spend a little more time with him. But as Timmy would tell you, one of the problems with me is that I don't show anything. I'm sure I never showed him how I felt or even told him. So he really had no idea. But I started feeling very positive about him around Christmas-time, because it was a long relationship to me. I mean the only other relationship I had before that time lasted maybe a month, with somebody in college.

And Christmas was weird because Timmy said he might go visit his sister, in Atlanta. I was still a certain distance from him as far as how I felt about him. There was more passion, but nowhere near how he felt about me.

Were you aware that he was a lot more involved with you, than you were with him?

Yes, yes I was, and it made me uncomfortable. The biggest feeling I had back then was that I was uncomfortable with everything. And I wanted my freedom. I had to have my freedom... I couldn't get involved with anybody... I just wanted to run around. 'Cause I was still new in New York and all that shit.

So Timmy said he might go away for Christmas....

Yeah... and I really wanted... I think I kind of hinted, as much as I thought I was allowed to, that we spend it together. I made the decision that I wasn't going to go back home. I had to prove to myself that I could spend Christmas without my family. And I also felt that I would like to spend it with Timmy and maybe get a little bit closer. Because I have those typical feelings around Christmas-time — you know, outpourings of emotion. Which for me isn't very much — even over Christmas — but it was still more than I normally ever did. I really thought that he was not going to go at one point, because he wasn't sure. But he did. It was a very last minute decision, the night before. And I was really heartbroken he did that. And I was angry.

Were you surprised you were heartbroken?

No. No, because when he told me he might go, I felt very bad and kind of angry that, uh, well gee, if he felt this way about me — and he kept telling me he did — shouldn't he want to spend Christmas with me? But he said he hadn't seen his sister in a long time. But I was very selfish then; I wasn't going to accept anything but Timmy spending Christmas with me. And when he didn't, I was angry. And Christmas Eve I went out to G.G. Barnum's, I was hanging around at G.G.'s a lot at that time, because of Johnnie — I was still seeing Johnnie too, off and on, which by Christmas had really gotten to be like maybe only once or twice a month, if that much. As a matter of fact, I had Johnnie make me a winter coat, which he finally finished on Christmas Eve, and I went up there, and we decided to go to G.G.'s for Christmas Eve. So I spent Christmas Eve with Johnnie Martinez and a Tuinal at a drag-queen/hustler bar.

It's a classic image.

Um . . . and at some point I met — there were two guys dancing, and I just went up to them and I started dancing with them. And um . . . I said would you like to have a threesome? And one said yeah.

Were you always that bold?

No, but when I'm on these drugs I get very loose.

So what did they say?

So one said sure, and then I asked the other and he said no, this guy's only a friend, we've tricked once but we've since become just friends. Oh . . . and this freaked me out: one guy turned out to be Jerry's employer! Jerry was the guy I was living with in Brooklyn Heights? And the other one was an architect, so it was an interior designer and an architect. And I spent Christmas Eve and Christmas morning with one guy and then I went home and showered and called up the other one and I spent Christmas afternoon with him. And so . . . I mean Christmas Day was a lot of sex. Because I was determined to forget about Timmy.

Did you succeed?

Ah... yeah. But then, I was going to Christmas Mass at St. Patrick's....

Between these two tricks?

Um... as a matter of fact I went from the one trick's apartment on the East Side to St. Patrick's. And that kind of fitted in, that the only place I could go to Christmas Mass was St. Patrick's. No other church would do. (Laughs) So I had that, but Christmas evening I went over to the model's apartment and spent the night there.

Now who was the model?

The model, the forty-year-old model. That I told you about?

Oh, so you had a third one?

Yeah. This was the model. Actually he was a former model.

Whom you were seeing at this time?

Yeah, so that fit in very nicely.

So you had sex with three people in twenty-four hours?

(Laughs) Yes.

Plus mass.

Plus mass. (Laughs) Yes, I needed the inspiration. To carry on. But there was a brief moment when I found myself saying, "What are you doing?" I mean this seemed so sacrilegious, you know. Popping in and out of bed on Christmas Day. I mean how could I possibly do this. At some point, of course, I called my family and wished them a merry Christmas.

From whose apartment?

(Laughs) From my own I think — yeah, cause it was in the daytime, it was when I was home between the first and second one, showering. (Laughs) But I was really determined to forget about Timmy on that day. And I think I could have. I felt very good that all this was happening and I felt occupied.

So you would. How long was Timmy away?

I think two days. He did call me when he came back, but I wasn't
very receptive. I don't remember much more except that we decided
to spend New Year's Eve together. New Year's Eve was fifty dollars
at Studio, but we decided to spend it cause Jerry and everybody were
getting into it. We were going to eat at a restaurant up here on the
West Side, the Café des Artistes. Jerry arranged all of this. At the
time he was the coordinator of activities for our little group. We had
friends coming in from Boston also who joined us. So our little group
had dinner up there and then went to Studio. And... oh, we
dropped acid before — Michel got acid for us. So that was fun. I
really felt good spending New Year's Eve with Timmy. And I lost all
of that animosity that I had toward him... though I think he was
kind of disappointed that we didn't go home together afterwards. I
went back home with Jerry, because I was really so hyped up. We
were so hyped up that Jerry and I went back and cleaned the whole
apartment New Year's Day. You know, we just couldn't go to sleep. I
don't know why I didn't spend the night with Timmy. But... I
thought it was wonderful that he was the first one I gave a kiss to in
1979 and all that kind of romantic crap. (Laughs)

Were you still seeing each other about once a week?

Yeah, I guess so. And at some point he said to me — we had a very
serious discussion in Brooklyn Heights, and I remember for the first
time I cried. I just really opened up to him and said, "You know, I
really can't communicate my emotions, my feelings. I just can't...
do it very well." And I saw him as being so good at it, he could
express everything so well.

Did he understand that?

Mmmm. I don't think so. No, I don't think he did. I told him I loved
him. And that was very difficult to say. Because I don't think I had
said "I love you" to anybody at all. God. Maybe one other person in
my whole life. That was something we never said at home to each
other, or to anybody else. I don't think he understood how hard it
was for me. A little later, when I suggested we move in together —
that I move in with him — he was just very calm and told me why he

thought it would be difficult. But I decided I had to move into Manhattan and I found this... *really* ratty apartment near him. But the neighborhood was scary, really terrible — it made Timmy's block look safe. But I wanted to prove something. And within a week of moving in I was robbed.

What was your reaction?

I was scared shitless. I really was. God. I called Timmy at the office. I was scared shitless for what was left of my things, which wasn't much. So... I started freaking out, you know — I called the telephone company and the electric and gas company and had everything turned off. I didn't care where I went, I was going to move out. Timmy said, "We have to get you out of there." He thought I was going to get killed. I didn't know whether I was gonna get killed, but I was frightened of what was going to happen next. So he spent the evening with me. He brought Roger over — Roger's the German shepherd — and I think Patti also came over with Minnie and Cha, the two other dogs, and Timmy stayed overnight with Roger. I was afraid someone was going to break in while I was there; that's why I pleaded with Timmy to bring Roger over and stay with me. The very next day — it was a beautiful, cool May day — Patti came with a car, and we moved everything to Fiftieth Street. I felt like I was being *rescued*, that I could breathe again. It was an incredibly good feeling. Despite that fact that I was moving into this zoo. But I didn't care because I was so glad to get out of that place.

So this incident got us living together. I was kind of excited about getting what I wanted, which was to have him live with me. But we talked about it and realized that we *weren't* living together, we were living with Patti in this community with all of these animals. And I immediately went about putting up lights, like in the bathroom, and doing little things to make life a bit more comfortable — putting up plants and things like that.

What was it like living with him?

Well, there was always a constant source for sex. And we never really had any problems that I could see. My only problem was with Patti. She was supposed to be in charge of paying the bills and she was negligent and she just seemed to be a very sloppy person. The conditions started to get to me after a while. So I tried to improve them. All we had between Patti's bedroom and ours was a drape, so we could carry on, but still she could hear us. So we decided that when Timmy got his money from the screen treatment, we were going to get doors, and I was going to fix up the apartment. 'Cause I was convinced that we could all live together. And if we got doors, Timmy and I would have our privacy. I got to the point where I drew up all these plans of how each room was going to look, and what the color scheme was gonna be and all that. (Laughs) Doing a designer number on this apartment in Hell's Kitchen. One room was going to be his office, I was going to put in a little closet. . . .

And you did buy the doors?

Yeah, we did. One door had soundproofing in it. They were real cheap doors, but that's all we could afford. The whole thing — the two doors and three sets of wooden bifolds for the windows — came to about $550 with tax. And Timmy kept joking about it, so for a while it was a sore spot with us that the doors cost so much. He was always bringing it up, saying, well you know, doors cost $500. And I felt bad about it, but I figured we had to buy doors for privacy. Also, it was my way of keeping the cats off of my bed and the hair away from me. 'Cause the hair was unbelievable. Everybody there was shedding, and the hair was *this* thick on the kitchen floor. And that's one thing that bothered me, Patti was not working and yet she was not cleaning up, and I was getting tired of her irresponsibility. Because she did not properly pay the telephone bill, we had our phone service cut off for a whole week, which was a tremendous inconvenience. There was absolutely no reason for it. She should have paid the bill. Period. She had a very nonchalant attitude towards life, and it was just a little bit too much for me. And Timmy seemed to be saying, "Well, that's Patti, that's the way she is. Nobody's ever going to change her, so you might as well accept it." But I was going to change things in the apartment — I really thought I could use my talent to make life better for them. That's why I went to all the trouble of getting the doors and the windows and putting these plants up. But I think Patti kind of resented it and Timmy felt that I was wasting my time or something. I don't know.

Did you get discouraged, thinking it would be hard for you to live together if your values were so different?

No.

No?

No, because I was falling more in love with him by the day.

How did that manifest itself?

Um, I think sex with him meant more, and I just felt much closer to him and . . . I mean, he had me very tired, he's very sexual. I don't know how he does it.

What does that mean? He likes sex more than once a day, or—

He probably would have me fuck him three times a day, if he could get away with it. But I can't do that. I have to be into it, you know. And, yeah, at that time he seemed more sexual than I did. He could just carry on forever. And we did. I think we were doing MDA at that time, too, and we had real long sessions. He doesn't like me to call them sessions, but I call them sessions. Hours and hours and hours, from like ten in the morning to three or four. We'd be carrying on with this MDA. And I guess it was when I started taking that drug that I really got into fucking him and when I really got into this role. And at first it was a role, but then I think I felt so comfortable with it, that it suddenly no longer was something I was doing to please Timmy, it was something that I was doing because I wanted to do it. And it worked out perfect — he loved it, and I was doing it because I wanted to do it. That's something we joke about a bit, that he really got me into fucking, and he said, "Now I have to watch you go out into the world and fuck everybody." Which is a sore spot with us.

Why? Because you do?

Yes. Or he thinks I do. But I told him before that if I go out dancing, which I love to do, and I meet somebody, fine, but I always come home. And he said, at one point, "Well, just remember, save the last dance for me."

So you were falling more in love with him?

Yeah.

And tension was building in the apartment between you and Patti?

Yes. He sensed it. We didn't know what to do about it. I got the feeling that he thought I was just living there temporarily till I could find
something. One night I said, "Well, you know, we really could all
live here and have a life together and everything," but I don't think
he was too convinced of that. I was, but I don't think he was. He said
something like, "Oh, well, we'll see what happens." But I had it in
my mind that we were definitely going to live together, for quite a
while.

**So for a while now it was Timmy who had been holding back — a
reversal of your first few months.**

Yeah. And it was only in Palm Springs that he really discovered
those things he had been hiding and holding back on for so many
years. I never understood that. I tried to have him explain it, but he
couldn't.

Let's go back. He went to Palm Springs in July?

Yes, as a matter of fact, he went around July second because he spent
July fourth in Malibu. He and Ray had gone for three weeks to finish
the screenplay. That was very difficult, those last few nights. I was
holding back because I didn't want to treat it like something real
serious. We talked about that, about him saying he was going off to
war. I said, "Really, Timmy," I said, "I don't want to think of this as
you going off to war, I just want to think of this as a temporary
thing." Because I was... I really felt horrible about him going away.
I saw it as a little breather in our relationship, you know, as something that probably would be good for us, to get away from each
other. But I was also really upset that he was leaving. I remember the
scene at the airport; it was real difficult saying goodbye to him
because I had this phobia about airline crashes and... strange things
like that were going through my mind. I thought he was only going
to be away for about a week, or two weeks at the very most. And we
spoke to each other every day, but that first night, um, I went to the
Ice Palace to try to forget, you know? And I couldn't.

To try to pick someone up?

Un, no, not... just to dance. I like to dance to take my mind off of things. If I meet somebody, that's fine, but even to talk to somebody... A lot of times you go there and you meet somebody just to talk to them and dance with them for the evening and you say good-bye. I guess I was looking again to forget, but in a much, much different way than Christmas Eve. I wanted to take my mind off it so much. But I remember sitting there and all of a sudden starting to cry because I couldn't take this. I missed him so much. I just started crying, and I left and went home and literally cried myself to sleep, just trying to forget him, but I couldn't go to sleep for the longest time. I was really, really upset. I mean, at... I... I think at that point I felt towards Timmy like I felt towards *no* one in my life. Even right now Timmy is closer to me than my family will ever be. And at that point he was the closest and dearest and most important thing in my life. And it frightened me — it really frightened me — that I felt this way about somebody, that it was having this effect on me, and having his control over me. And, you know, a lot of times, I was saying, hold back, take it easy, don't get so involved. But I couldn't help it. I was loving it and being afraid of it at the same time, so it was really that head-over-heels kind of true love stuff. (Pause)

After a while, I realized he was not going to be in California for two weeks but for a longer time and I started changing my way of looking at it. So the uncomfortableness of his absence was diminished, and I was kind of getting back into the routine of things. I knew I couldn't live thinking like that and worrying all the time; I just had to start getting back into living in New York rather than saying, well, when is he going to come home? Because he never knew when he was gonna come home. He always said, "Well, I don't know... we don't know how long we're gonna be." So after about two weeks I realized he's gonna be there longer than I thought, and I better get used to him being away, because it's probably gonna happen in the future, and I kept saying this is all very good for us and everything.... So I just resigned myself to the situation.

Would you describe the two of you, at this time, as "lovers"?

Yes, by that time. After I had proposed to him — that we live together, I mean, in March — and we began talking about how we felt about each other and he realized how strongly I'd begun to feel about him, we decided we should use the term *lover*. We both felt comfortable with it.

Tell me about California. How did you finally decide to go out there?

Oh, Timmy called me up and said, "Are you sitting down?" And I said "Yes, why?" (I was standing up actually, but it didn't matter.) And he said, "We decided that we want you to come out here. Would you be able to come to California?" I couldn't believe it. I was going to be able to go to California and see Timmy — it was just too much.

I felt kind of uneasy about going into that situation, with them working. But I really wanted to see Timmy. It was really overwhelming. So I made all the plans and went out.

What was it like to be there?

I was so nervous that day, and the flight out was just so long. I had a layover in Los Angeles which was boring, and the trip from Los Angeles to Palm Springs seemed to take forever. It was just a wonderful feeling when we landed and I got out and this hot, hot air hit me. It must have been ninety degrees, and it was eight o'clock in the evening. As it happened, the plane dropped us off at the farthest end of this tiny airport. And I was one of the last out of the plane, so it took a long time for me to make my way through the airport. And it was just an incredible feeling seeing him standing on the other side of the doors, by the luggage area, waiting for me. He had on what I call his sex kitten shorts (laughs) — he had those tattered shorts on. And a T-shirt, and he was very tanned and he looked wonderful. He looked just wonderful. And we were — temporarily — just slightly *awkward*, because we were in the airport, but we hugged each other and carried on. It was wonderful.

Did you kiss each other in the airport?

Yes, of course. By that time I had gotten to the point where I could kiss Timmy anywhere. I didn't give a fuck who saw. Kissing Timmy meant more to me than any reaction I might have gotten from anybody on the street. Yeah, I kissed him and hugged him and held his hand. It was very obvious... we were very, very obviously gay. But I didn't care at all. And it meant a lot for me to do that, because of how I felt about showing emotion in public and particularly expressing any kind of so-called *gay* behavior in public.

What was the house like?

I really didn't know what to expect. He had told me there was a larger house a little farther up on the hill, and they were using the pool house. Which I thought was strange — that they weren't using the main house. But when I got there, I saw this beautiful Spanish-type house that was shaped like a very wide V, with different colored lighting around the landscaping. In front was a kidney-shaped pool that was beautifully blue. There was a warm breeze blowing, and it was just wonderful, like wow! (chuckles) And it was very nice inside. Clean, very California, and very, very cool. I felt a little bit awkward at first, but Ray was nice about everything. And he was very casual. They had the charcoals on and we were going to have hamburgers.

Who cooked?

Ray did all the cooking. He was a wonderful cook.

So how was life there with them?

Timmy wanted me to keep the same routine they did, which was stay up late and go to bed at dawn. But I found out quickly that's something I couldn't do. So I just went to bed early. I slept very well, and I slept a long time. And then Timmy would eventually come to bed. And I'd put my arms around him right away, and we'd fall asleep that way. I would usually be the first one up in the morning; they would get up around noon or one. And it became a routine: being in the pool, sometimes they would write in the afternoon, a late dinner, and always coffee and coke by the pool looking up at the beautiful sky, which was always clear at night. With the crickets. It was just wonderful. Any hour of the night, we'd all just strip down and swim. We never had sex in the pool — that's one thing we didn't do. We had sex beside the pool. But the water was ninety-five degrees, and just being in the water with Timmy and holding him and everything was wonderful.

The water was ninety-five degrees?

Yeah, it was fabulous, particularly in the evening. And the sex was just incredible too; the sex was marvelous. The companionship. I mean we had no problems, no problems in the world. New York was just a million miles away. Patti was a million miles away. Even though I wanted to talk about it, he just kept putting it off. Obviously because he was having such a good time. He didn't want to talk about anything serious. We were really turned on to each other. Even more than in New York, I think. Everything was so wonderful there. Listening to Dolly Parton. The dinners. The whole thing. The dishwashers, the color television sets, all that stuff — you know, to us who lived on Fiftieth Street in dire poverty — was wonderful. That's where Timmy started appreciating and accepting luxuries in life. And wanting them. And at some point I realized talking to him that he was really serious about us finding a place together and moving out. After he had found out about the arguments back in New York, he just wanted to get me out to California, away from Patti, because she was acting very strange. Very, very inconsistent. That's all he was concerned about at that time. Then he really started developing — thank God — an appreciation of the finer things in life. Or even the bare necessities. For that, I was grateful.

He felt he could live comfortably?

Yeah. And accept it. I think he had this idea that he couldn't accept these things, he wasn't comfortable with them, they didn't fit into his life — whatever. But at some point in Palm Springs he decided — as he put it — he was doing all this hard work writing and thinking and that he found it very comfortable to go to these luxuries for pleasure. And just enjoy and appreciate them for what they were. I always felt that he deserved these things, and why shouldn't he have them? Why shouldn't he enjoy them? There's no harm in it. But it took him a while to think that.

So in Palm Springs, you were totally clear to yourself that you were in love with him?

Uh-huh. And that I could live with him for a very long time.

And did you two discuss it?

Yeah.

Had you by now found it easy to tell your emotions to him?

Yeah. Yeah. 'Cause his absence really made me think about a lot of
things, and I decided that I could live with this guy. I could make a
commitment to him. But he wasn't really sure whether he could
make a commitment to me. He didn't know. And to this day I'm still
more confident than he is about that. I don't know whether he's
afraid I'm going to run off with a trick or something like that, or
whether he just can't commit himself. But I think it's a gradual thing,
and I'm at the point now where I'm very confident about it.

**So now that you plan to live together where does it stand with out-
side sex and outside involvement?**

Well, as far as I'm concerned, I have no outside involvement. As I
said, the outside sex occurs if somebody is interested.

Is it as good as your sex with Timmy?

No. It's just fucking, that's all it is. I kind of put it on the same level
as, um, going to the movies with somebody. It's just another
experience. Somebody turns me on, they're turned on to me, we do
it, it's sex, and that's it. But I have a feeling that Timmy feels
threatened by it. And I have a vein of jealousy running through me,
if I think he's carrying on with somebody. But I'm a Scorpio.
(Laughs) We're supposed to be that way. But I am that way,
anyway.

Do you expect to allow him to do that, or. . . ?

Yes. I think if he's doing it, he's doing it for a reason. Either because
he thinks he's not getting enough from me, or he has urges that are
overwhelming, or he likes somebody sexually, physically, whatever,
to the point that he wants to have sex with them. I think it's fine. But
I do have a little bit of jealousy. If I think about it.

So you don't want to hear about that?

Right. I don't want to hear about it. I don't press it. We've always
said that it's something that we probably would do and that we

wouldn't talk about. This goes back a long time, to when we were only dating and we were carrying on with other people. If it's ever brought up, I say that I meet very nice people. That seems to bother him, that I could possibly meet nice people, even though they're only tricks. He seems to think I should only deal with them as sexual objects, and not as people. But I can't be that way. If I meet people, it's because I *like* them — you know, not only physically but their personality as well. I can spot a mile away someone who is just out to have sex with me. If you go to the Mineshaft or a backroom bar you know what everybody's there for, you don't have to worry about personalities. But if you're dancing and somebody comes up to you, and you start talking and hit if off, then lots of times a logical sequence, for me, is to have sex with them. Then that's that, and then you say good-bye.

Have you ever met each other when you're out separately?

No. That would freak me out. Studio is the only place we've ever gone singly and met, but not since March did that ever happen. I thought I might see him at the Cock Ring last night, because he was working late. I was at the Ring, and he said that he often likes to stop off there after work. I was looking for him, but he wasn't there.

Do you feel threatened by the fact that he may trick, or just jealous?

It's a little bit of jealousy, to think that somebody's fucking my man (laughter) but he says it's just an impersonal thing. So I'm taking it from what he says and going along with the fact that it's just typical gay sex, where there's no involvement — just out for the pleasure. You know: just to come. But I don't get the feeling that he's comfortable with me doing it. Which is something — we have to work on that. We have to work on that.

Do you think there are other major things you have to work on?

No. Except one thing which has been ongoing, my inability to express emotions towards him. That's something I have to work on. And he has admitted that I have made some headway as far as that's concerned. It's becoming more a part of my personality. Since I've known him, I have changed drastically, I've turned into ah... he's really turned me into a fucker. (Laughs) I guess that's how you put it.

I've always been an aggressive person and I've always been in conflict with my sexuality being passive. In the sense that I was a right pocket. Before this.

What?

Right pocket is the passive, meaning: likes to get fucked. The keys on the right side, that kind of thing. I've changed to putting the handkerchief over here, in the left pocket.

I never could keep them straight.

But it's very strange. As far as being an aggressive personality, it worked out fine that I turned into being this way. I never liked to be fucked, so I can simply say now, No, I don't get fucked. And that's it. And interestingly enough, the handkerchiefs have proven effective in keeping away those kinds of people. Which I find fascinating. It has really kept away those kinds of people.

How do you feel about Timmy's work? When you met him, he looked like a street person and had a clerical position, but in the past year, he's written a screenplay, got paid many thousands of dollars. How does that . . . ?

Well, I've always felt that he was extremely intelligent and didn't deserve to be doing the schlep work he did. It bothered me constantly that he was doing this. I kept saying to him, "Well, why don't you try to do something else. Get out of there if you're not satisfied." And I guess he would tell me the same thing when I complained about my job. I am extremely happy that this has happened to him because to me it's this justification, it's like what goes around, comes around. Right now he's where he should be, and the things happening to him, he deserves. When I read the screenplay, I was taken aback by the depth and the intelligence and the . . . the artistry of it. It was wonderful, thinking that my Timmy was doing this. My entire life I've always admired people who have done things more than properly, done things to the point of genius. I respected that very much and I told him so.

So you don't foresee any problems if he becomes successful and well-known?

You mean jealousy or something like that?

Yes.

I only want good things for him. I know he can handle them and I know he won't be overwhelmed by them because he's just not that kind of person. I'm absolutely confident that whatever happens to him, he's going to direct it, he's going to control it. He's extra-ordinary. I think he's an extraordinary person.

Where are you in your own work at this point?

Well, I totally broke off relations with Jerry and the design job we were doing together, so my first design job turned out to be a disaster because I had to legally write myself out of it. I learned a lot from that and shortly after I got another design job, and we're in the process of finishing it now. I'm confident that I want to be a designer and that I can handle the pressure. And most importantly, I'm my own boss, and that's something I can live with. I can be responsible for my own mistakes and my own success.

So you don't see any problem for the foreseeable future?

No. As far as my career goes, I know it's gonna take time for me. And Timmy's not the kind of person that throws up success to you, so you couldn't possibly dislike him for it or become envious of him.

Does he take an interest in your work?

Yes. I think as much as anyone could expect him to be interested, he is. He doesn't understand it all — it's not something that he's really involved in. Until we visited Palm Springs he was never even interested in nice things. So I can't imagine him being too interested in color schemes or paint swatches — he jokes to me about my paint swatches and all those kinds of things. . . . I don't know, I guess in a way he thinks it's funny that people find all this very necessary, you know. That I'm spending my life making this necessary. Because I'm not really making social statements or doing anything earth-shattering. It's a very ephemeral kind of profession to be in. I guess I could make statements if I want, but not at this point in my life.

What does Timmy mean to you now?

What does Timmy mean to me now? Give me time to think.

O.K. We actually have a pause button on this machine.

(Laughs) No, I think these blank spaces are fine. I don't mind the spaces. Humm, well, as I told him, he is *the* person in my life. It's very strange, I always tell him Never say *never*, but I kind of don't want anybody else in my life at this time. And the only way that I could ever perceive him leaving my life is through the death of one of us. In that sense, it's a very heterosexual kind of thing, the marriage-till-death-do-us-part kind of thing. I mean, God knows what's going to happen, but at least making that statement is something I can do at this point because I want to, and I feel confident saying it. To spend the rest of my life with him.

What do you feel about his emotional commitment to other people like Ray or his close friends?

Well, I feel they're important, as I think that the success of our relationship is going to depend on the ability of both of us to maintain friendships outside of the marriage, to keep things going outside, so that we have our individuality, our own pursuits, but still are able to come together, as two people can.

You don't have the feeling that you have to be everything to each other?

No, I feel very much *against* being everything to Timmy. I think he should have his own life as much as possible, and even his own friends if he wants. We can have mutual friends, certainly. But I think that if two people mean too much to each other, there's going to be a lot of problems, they become *too* dependent on each other and there's no breathing space. I've talked to him about tension between two people, tensile forces being necessary between people. It's like when, during the mating process, they used to put two gorillas in a cage, a male and female, and they would never mate. As soon as they put a wall between the two of them, but gave them space to see each other, they were able to become sexually aroused and mate. It's only because there has to be a certain tension there. Also in the most successful marriages — I think they've done studies on it — people don't have so much in common, they have other pursuits, and they don't always get along tremendously. And I know I'm not going to get along all the time with Timmy. I know there's going to be arguments and all that stuff. You see what I'm saying? There's going to be that friction there. . . .

Sure. . . you want to go to Bloomingdale's and he wants to go to Orchard Street.

(Laughs) Yes. And we overcome those things by joking about them, and by giving in. For instance, he got his hair cut at Vidal Sassoon, and I went down to Canal Street to buy jeans — little things like that. We decided that that's what we're going to have to do, we're going to have to give in on things. And compromise. I think we're both willing to compromise.

Okay. How do you feel about Timmy? You used traditional heterosexual terms a lot to describe your relationship, so I wanted to try to get at that. What's the tonality of your feelings?

Well, he used to give me Kurt Vonnegut to read, and Vonnegut spoke a lot about common decency, people having common decency for each other. We talked about that a lot, how that's probably more important than having love for somebody. Because oftentimes you do things out of love and you wind up hurting someone. You love somebody so much that you don't even think about their feelings, you think about the love of it all, and as a result you wind up hurting them. So we both feel that for the best relationship, common decency has to come first. That's a strange thing, talking about common decency — like, what is common decency? I don't know if I really know, except that we are trying to find out together, you know, the limits of common decency, and you kind of find out by trial and error. If you do something for love and if it hurts, then you can't do it again. Respect has a lot to do with it. Respect for the person's feelings. And that's what we're working on, trying to have respect for each other and a commonly decent attitude towards each other. With love mixed in. Love is in there too. We're making conscious efforts not to hurt each other. . . .

So it's an amalgam of feelings, like romantic love, at times like. . .

Buddies.

Playing together?

Yeah. Because I tease him a lot, or smack him, or wrestle — stuff like that. Childish things, being silly with each other, yeah. He calls me his baby man. Because he thinks I remind him of a little boy and at the same time a man. I call him my baby doll or something like that, too. Because sometimes, he's so precious to me that I think of him as a little helpless baby in the sense of how extremely lightly I have to tread with his emotions. You know, I grew up in a house where there were no holds barred; when you spoke to somebody, you went to the crux of it and really insulted the person. So I have to pull that back and be very careful about how I speak to him. And that's something I have to work on. I've been rude at times. And tacky at times. It's something I have to work on.

It's only in the last couple of months that we've really played around with each other, or joked around each other. But he's very quick with his mind, Timmy is, very challenging; he'll come back to you with a really good answer, which I like. He's very alert.

So this relationship is now making you very happy?

Oh, yeah.

Is it as important as your work?

It's more important. Yeah. . . . I mean the most important thing in my life up until Timmy was being a designer, making it, living in a good apartment, dressing well. But he made me realize that all of that is second. If he didn't *make* me realize it, I realized it through him — that the most important thing to me is loving him and being with him. I mean, it's evident in how I dress now, my attitude towards everything. And that's important to me, that I realize what I was, that what I was was wrong to a certain extent. That I got where I am now, Timmy is responsible for. I mean everybody knows what the image of Studio conjures up, the plasticity of it all. And I was really into that plasticity of the New York night life and all that bullshit and dressing up. If I dress up now, I call it my D and D drag — *D and D* is the Decoration and Design Building where all of the fabric and furniture outlets are — I just dress up now when I have to go there and present myself.

More importantly, he's made me realize that having a relationship with someone is important, because I gave up a lot of freedom, or what I perceived as being freedom: living by myself. Accomplishing things by myself was really important for me at one time, but now I'm thinking in terms of *us*. *Us* getting an apartment, *us* doing this, *us* accomplishing these things together. Because I guess I realized that I really probably need somebody to help me do these things. And to live my life. I need somebody to help me live my life. And he came across as the perfect person. I would just be a fool not to realize that. I mean, many people would say, "Well, I'll meet somebody better later on." But I don't have that hope that I would ever meet anybody better than Timmy. And I don't want to take that chance. It's too risky. Again, it's like the traditional heterosexual way of looking at things: you meet somebody and you're content with them and you're happy and maybe you live together for a while and you decide to get married because it's what you want. And this is what I want.

TIMMY

How did you meet Robert — when and where?

We met in a backroom of the Stud in August 1978. It was on Thursday night — for some reason I remember that. I was standing in the Stud and I saw this guy. He looked young, he had a beard — a young beard but it was a beard and I like beards — and he had a weird sort of shirt on. Fashion in images means a lot to me when I cruise, and this was not just a T-shirt, this was more than a T-shirt — it was an interpretation of the T-shirt.

Like what you're wearing now?

No. This is a legitimate football jersey — see, it has room for shoulders. I have no shoulders, but it has room for shoulders — or shoulder pads. I suspect just shoulders though, from the size of it. But he also had jeans on and construction boots. So he was about 70/30 — 70 percent normal faggot that I can interpret immediately, 30 percent a little bit weird. He was cruising me aggressively, and I was coquetting, because I wasn't sure about him. And I had just gotten there, I think. Anyway, he came over to me, put his hand on my crotch and that was sufficiently aggressive to turn me on. So we moved to one of the brick walls on the far side and we had very democratic, pleasurable sex. I probably got to his cock first — I usually do — but he went down on me too, and I went down on him, and he went down on me. And this went on for quite a while, until it got too hot and we both came; then we went into the front room to cool off. And he was not leaving — most people just leave — but he also wasn't saying anything. So I started talking to him, and we decided it was too hot and horrible there, so we were both going to leave. We walked to Hudson Street, and he *still* wasn't leaving. He walked me up to Fourteenth Street, not talking, but for some reason I was talking enough that night. And it had been such pleasurable sex — really pleasurable — the feeling, even sexually, was that this was a nice person. As I said, it was very democratic, it was not polar sex like S & M . . . .

You mean it was reciprocal?

Yeah. And at some point I asked him if he wanted to come back to Fiftieth Street, because I was relaxed with him by that time and talking easily and making jokes. I could see that he couldn't quite get a lot of the jokes and that he wasn't doing too much talking — I had to ask him questions and draw him out — and I found out immediately about his Studio 54 trip. That made me suspicious, because usually I look for something different, not just a West Village fag, or a Studio 54 fashion freak, or a decorator queen on the Upper West Side who never goes outside the ring of bars up here. But I guess I found something that was different. Or maybe I was just flattered that he was not leaving, that he seemed to want to stay with me. In any case I brought him back to Fiftieth Street, to the hellhole. I warned him, as I've warned everybody who's ever been there, that there was nothing but animals and litter and hair and tenements. But we went up on the roof for a while, and it's real nice up on the roof. The roof is romantic. And we had more reciprocal as you say, democratic as I say, sex on the roof.

At the time, I was going over lots of real life hurdles. I had decided I was leaving Ray's employ but I hadn't told him yet, which was very nerve-racking for me, so for a couple of weeks I didn't follow up on a personal life in any way at all. I had lots of sex, lots of people and phone numbers in the drawer, but never called them. He called me once, but I didn't get the message. Then he called again and he said, "This is Robert . . . Do you remember me? We met at the Stud." I said, "How could I forget you?" because it was memorably the most pleasant human sexual experience I'd had... in that period of time.

In that period of time?

I couldn't say ever because I hadn't thought about it that much, but it was remarkably nice, remarkably pleasant. It was not so easy to objectify him sexually, he wasn't an older guy with dark hair and mustache and flannel shirt and jeans. It's almost as if I were forced to deal with the person from the start because the person was not my ideal image, but I was attracted to him anyway. So that's how we met.

I don't remember what we did the second time we met. I guess we stayed at my house, but I went to Brooklyn very soon after that, and he was living in an equally weird situation, in one room with this flipped out fashion queen, who was really a drag queen not out of the closet. Miss Jerry could roll her sleeves up and iron everything — iron and iron and *iron* — they had clothes all over the place and shoes and shoeboxes and... I was just leaving that world, I was leaving the fashion business... (long pause) and yet that's when sleeping with Robert and cuddling with him became terribly important. He's a wonderful cuddler.

So you started going to Brooklyn?

Yeah, because it was hard to be cuddly in my apartment. Which was not warm, it was always cold, always stark — it was not comfortable. The apartment in Brooklyn — in spite of how weird it was having this other nutty person in the same room with us — in spite of that it was very warm, and that's when I became aware of the pleasure of sleeping with him, the pleasure of just cuddling with him.

How old were you then?

Twenty-four.

Where were you emotionally when you met Robert?

I had left Jay about five months, six months before, I had lived with him for two and a half years. I was extremely cynical about lovers and relationships. I was not in a secure position because of my job. I had also just moved into an apartment with my friend Patti. And I was still cynical about the first love affair I had when I was nineteen with Timothy, an Englishman... that was about a year of pain in my life, because I couldn't accept the withdrawal of this sudden passion. I had been really swept away by that... by my own romanticized image of a relationship with a man, which is a complication of the white picket fence, television commercials, books I had read, etc. I think it runs the gamut from serious to absolutely silly, this image I had of a relationship with a lover. Ummm, a male lover because I never considered having a female lover; even when I was very, very young. I knew I wanted a man and would have to get one. So I do remember sounding very cynical the night I met Robert.... That was the defense I was employing, because of the horrible relationship with Jay, which was not terribly upsetting to me, because I always understood it. But the relationship way back, the one six years ago when I was eighteen, is still the one that moves me and confuses me. Because that's the one that was about passion — about taking a chance and giving myself totally away. I've learned since then that you can't give yourself totally away, that's just not possible on this planet. You know, people are not characters in fairy tales. When you give yourself too much, it creates an imbalance, you have a hole in you, somebody else has too much of you and they don't know what to do with it. Although the passion I experienced in that first affair was so heightened, and such total pleasure for me, I do feel now that that's not appropriate — the price is too high. I guess I've spent the last six years either protecting myself from that or looking for it and not finding it. And those were the only two relationships I've had since I was seventeen, which was the point at which I became sexual. Anything else I don't count because *I* was never involved — even if somebody else fell in love with me, or something like that, *I* was not involved.

Did you think that Robert was your age or younger? Did that make any difference?

I thought he was young — which he was, twenty-two to my twenty-four — and I was not accustomed to having sex with people younger than me... because they usually didn't make the move. And it took — and takes — well no, not any more, but at that time I think it really took aggression from someone to turn me on. Once I was turned on, then I was very aggressive about whatever I was doing, whatever role I was playing, but it took aggression from someone else to get me going. So yeah, I looked at him and thought he was younger than me. This is kind of weird. Things with younger people never work out, but things with older people never work out either, so what's the big difference? When we met, it was sex to me. And when we became involved with each other then it didn't matter that he was younger. Because age doesn't matter at all. But he was certainly not at the place that most of the people I had ever looked for or been involved with were at. He was not at all intellectual. He was not academic. He was not artsy. He was not even a freak of any kind. He seemed to me very normal, and yet what he was doing was courageous.

What was he doing?

Well, he had moved from Philadelphia. He was living with this horrible person. He was sticking it out. He was plugging away in the Big Apple. I thought that was very courageous and I admired that. We had nothing in common when we met — not even movies because I didn't like movies then. I'm still real snobby about movies. So we had nothing in common. And somehow that didn't seem to matter.

But there was a big style difference between you?

Oh yeah.

How would you describe the difference?

Well, he was into clothes. A lot of clothes. You know, a different look... for different things. And by that time I had developed only one look, my funky, streety look. I was working on that. Umm... my look has to do with looking kind of like a street punk. Because for one thing I feel safer looking like this. Still not easy, because I always know I look like a faggot too. But somehow I express a certain cool through the image I wear. And I did feel that anybody who went to Studio 54 and waited outside — either to be let in thankfully, or turned away for some stupid reason — was an asshole. I would never do it and I thought it was degrading and humiliating to the people who did. I also thought clothes to that extent were silly — frivolous.

Did you ever go to Studio yourself?

Only on the magic carpet ride — the silver spoon ride. I only went when the occasion was there, when I had nothing else to do — and it was a free ride all the way. Going in with Ray means going through the front door and not paying. There was tons of free drugs, and that's the reason I went. I went because it was big — and because there were drugs. But I was always bored there because I can't carry myself through dancing a whole night like so many other people can. What seems to me to be the turn-your-mind-off-and-dance-for-five-hours-thing that faggots do, I can't do. So whenever I went to Studio 54, I was bored, because the conversation was never thrilling — unless it was a night that Ray and I were hanging out together and just talking and looking. The drugs were always wonderful, so I took the drugs and I would just sit there. There was no cruising there ever, at all. And I don't know what to do in an environment where I can't cruise. That's what I have done for years and years. I've cruised. I don't care where I've been — on the train, in an office — I've gone through life cruising. And I don't know what the rest of these people are doing. And that was and still is a gap between Robert and me.

So he called you the second time... and then?

We started seeing each other.... I don't remember a lot about it. I don't remember how often we would see each other. I think what did it was when I started working for a card company. I was in the Village at least three or four days a week and I always had the opportunity to stop by The Storehouse where he worked. It was really the visits to The Storehouse that brought us together. They were only fifteen minutes or so, three times a week, but that's a time in which you can talk and become comfortable with somebody, though it wasn't a heavy sexual scene. I guess we were having sex about once a week or so. I'm not sure about that.

Were you pursuing him? Was he pursuing you? Who was keeping it going?

Well, I was courting him at the time because I was the one who, you know, had the job on the beat. I was the one who would go into the store. And after doing this for about a month or so — maybe even two months — I began to get that I-have-a-hole-in-me-somewhere feeling. I've been putting too much into this and I'm not getting anything back. There was no natural way then for him to contact me because I was always walking in to see him. When I was transferred from the card company to the magazine, I was never free anymore during the day and those little visits stopped. Uhmmm... almost everything stopped. 'Cause he was not making any moves. He wasn't contacting me more than, say, once a week. And he was not acting very interested. But by that time I had become very interested because we had been having these little visits for a long time. So it was hard for me. I felt, I'm slipping into something, I'm interested, very interested in this person. I'm feeling somewhat involved with him and doing all the work and getting nothing back. Uhmm... And I couldn't figure out how to talk to him about this. He seemed to want to just chat about television and go to sleep early. He never seemed to want to talk. And I've always been wary of this kind of "gay man" — I say that out of respect, because it's Robert I'm talking about, but "faggot" is the word — wary of the kind of faggot who never talks because he never thinks. And... I'm conscious of being maybe too serious, too weighed down sometimes. You know, not able to just cut off a serious line of thought and relax in easy chatter. I've always envied that too — faggots who could do that, who were good at that. But I couldn't do it. If something was on my mind and it wasn't somehow talked out or resolved, it was just on my mind. I couldn't shut it off and do something else. So, I would get this weird feeling when I was at his house, because he'd be chattering or watching television or something, and I just felt *nothing is going on here*. There were things I was unhappy about, but I was afraid to come out with them because I was afraid of being looked at like I was a Martian or something. Like I was talking a different language. 'Cause I've been terribly afraid of opening myself up and saying I feel this way and having somebody say, "What are you getting heavy on me for?" That was pretty much Robert's attitude at the time: "Aw, come on, let's not get heavy." To me it wasn't heavy because to me it was very lightening. Because if I said what I felt, I felt lighter.

Uh-huh.

Uhmm . . . But he seemed already to be light, so he didn't need that. So I often left in the morning feeling frustrated.

Yet you were getting more and more involved. *Something* **was involving you.**

Yeah. It was the warmth. It was the contact. It was this snuggling, non-threatening person who demanded nothing of me. You know, sleeping at night with a warm body, fitting very intimately and very closely in with it physically. That's what I was getting out of it. It was non-threatening to me, he demanded nothing of me and he gave me this warmth. I didn't have to protect myself against anything, which was wonderful, 'cause what I had come from was only relationships with these powerful personalities. In the end, they usually turn out to be not powerful people but weak people. But the pounding that I had gotten from Jay, uh, I never wanted to experience that again. I never wanted anybody to assault me emotionally, and this was the furthest possible thing from assault.

And the sex was fine. It was not — it was always erotic to me, but it was not an erotic scene, you know? But I was getting erotic scenes elsewhere, so that wasn't terribly important. This person was the only person I had met in a long time who I could relax and experience that warmth and intimacy with. And, yeah, I was kicking and screaming because I didn't feel anything else, but it was important to me at that time, very important, or else I wouldn't have done it. To feel safe in that one way. He in no way wanted to demolish me or overpower me or persuade me or affect me. In any way. So that's what made me go back, that's what made it really important to me.

So when did things come to a head?

On his birthday. I had wanted to get him something very special. I had set up an expectation for myself to find something very, very special for him that he would love. I guess I wanted to get through to him. I wanted to say, this much I have perceived about you. I really wanted the gift to work. And we were pretty close, seeing each other maybe twice a week by that time. By close, I mean comfortable. We had both accepted the fact that we were going to see each other on a regular basis for a while. I guess we were still dating or something.

So. He loved antelopes, deco antelopes, impalas, things like that.

And I went all over the city looking for some special thing but I could only find tacky things. I couldn't find anything that was special and beautiful, and affordable. I could have gone to Steuben or someplace if I'd had lots of money and bought something extravagant that I would accept as beautiful. Eventually I found Bill Cunningham's book *Facades*, and I thought: well, this is fabulous. He's really interested in architecture and he's a fashion freak — by this time I had accepted the fashion freak because I liked it in him. I liked his sensibility; I respected it. He does it well. And although I was on the rebound from that myself, I could still really appreciate somebody who did it well. So I thought this is the perfect gift. And I really felt that it would give him a clue to me also. So I was thrilled about the book and I think I got him something else, maybe *The Language of Cats and Other Stories* by Spencer Holst. But that was for a different reason, that was because I thought it was something everybody should read. That kind of imagination is something he should be able to enjoy. Ummm... So I was real excited about the birthday present.

And then I made a card and footprinted all the animals — I signed the card from the whole house — and then I signed another card, a very special, beautiful, Oriental rice paper card, from me. And I wrote something in it. I wrote... I don't remember what I wrote, but it was sufficiently vague and sufficiently heavy to suffice.

How many animals did you have at this time?

Many, many, many. Must have been six cats and four dogs by that time. No. Maybe Harry hadn't come yet. But anyway, it was a ton of animals. Really a lot. And I thought: Well, at least this is a way to make light of this loony bin. So anyway, I got there and that night I was with Roger and that night also—

Roger was the German sheperd?

Yeah. He still is. That was the night of the gay march to Foley Square to protest the City Council incident. Whatever it was.... I don't even remember what it was now.

Rejecting the gay rights bill?

But I don't remember where is was — was it in the Committee or was it in the Council, or? — I don't remember which exact thing it was, but it was an angry night, and I was real involved in that and I wasn't going out dancing. He had invited me to go to Studio with him and his friends, and I knew I couldn't do that cause I couldn't bear his friends. Him I could deal with. But them I couldn't deal with at all, you know. To me they were just silly people.

So I got to the store, and they had had this whole little party, and he was real stoned. He was into angel dust then — uh — which I have to remind him of whenever he comes down on me for taking too many drugs, 'cause I was never an angel duster and that's severely stupid, and peculiar to faggots, disco faggots. It's a really stupid drug to take. And he came up out of the basement with this guy I had never seen before, and the guy had no shirt on and they were hanging all over each other and I . . . my face dropped.

You thought they'd been making out in the basement?

Uh-huh. So I was shocked and, like, "pierced through the heart" by that. But I quickly recovered my face — and my heart — and said, "Okay, the important thing here is that I'm going off to this demonstration tonight, and here's the gift." But he was so stoned that he had no real contact with me or the gift. He opened it and he said, "Oh, that's nice, that's sweet," and he kissed me . . . but he was much too stoned to be aware of the thought that went into it . . . and it just made me feel awful. I felt like it was a whole disaster that I had set myself up for. That was the first time that I felt, oh my God, I have these expectations, and they're just — snap! — crumbling in front of my eyes and I'm feeling pain again. Feeling fucking pain with a person. Also at that time I was only doing busywork on the magazine. My mind was doing nothing, so everything of that nature became enlarged. When I got to work in the morning, this was all I could think about while I was doing that inane work — labels and phone calls and fulfilling orders. My mind was not being used by anything else, so it was being eaten up and tormented by these things. Ummm . . . I find that happens less now because I have more important work in my life. And that's a good thing because I don't quite understand the torment. I'm very suspicious of . . . it's a reservoir of masochism I have that . . . you know I have these systems of tormenting myself, and I haven't yet crushed them. But at the same time, I felt legitimate about these feelings; I felt I was much more involved than he was. I was putting more thought into it, more attention, more time. And all of that was true. So I had a *real* angry march that night. Which renewed me in a certain way. I felt wonderful because it was a very angry, controlled crowd. And it was great to have that to rely on because it was the opposite of Studio and all those silly people. With the marchers, the fist-in-the-air dykes — those were the people who made me feel somehow solid again. So that was the birthday incident, and that was in November.

And things went on like that. I tried to talk to him about it. But it was real hard because whenever I would talk, the look would come over his face: "Oh, shit, he's getting heavy again." It was so frustrating I wanted to shake him and scream and yell: this is not heavy, you know; this is not college! I'm not coming in your dormitory room and laying a heavy trip on you — this is life, this is what it's about! But somehow I never did that. I'm not — or I wasn't then — emotionally equipped to just come out and say that. I was afraid that maybe he was gonna say, "Yes, yes it is — this is college to me," or . . . (pause) I'm not sure why I was afraid, but I was real afraid to say that and I never did. So we used to have these ridiculous roundabout conversations where I would not be able to just flat out explain to him what was bothering me. So that led to more frustration. And around Christmas—

Had you planned to spend Christmas together, originally?

Yeah. And as Christmas drew closer, I was really frustrated, really upset by the lack of communication between us. I couldn't just have this conversational chatter anymore. And he was really resisting anything more serious, anything heavier. I felt like I was moving in too quickly, and he was holding me at arm's length. And I couldn't bear that. It was very hard on my ego.

I began to feel that I was wasting my time. But what I really couldn't bear was being held at this distance. Because I don't threaten anybody in that way. I never demanded anything of him. I never asked him not to go out with his friends. I only said, "I prefer not to go out with you and your friends." The time I spent with his friends was always boring to me. It was as boring as the time with Ray's friends. There are just so many people who interest me, and that's not a great number. Ummm... so a lot of the time we were spending together he wanted to spend with his friends *and* me. And I think he thought I was being real snobby. And I was. (Laughs) Uh... but I couldn't bear his friends at all. I wanted time for me. Let him have his friends — please, take them, as Henny Youngman says, *but go.* When you spend time with me, I want attention to me, and I thought that was not unreasonable. And he was reacting to all sorts of things. I guess he had an affair going on... and he thought I was a threat to that, which I was not, because—

He had an affair going on around Christmas?

Yeah. Or maybe he was just having more sex then and he thought I was threatening that. But I really wasn't threatening anything. All I was doing was saying, "Please communicate with me. I want to be close to you." And he was holding me off.

His having an affair with someone else didn't threaten you?

Not then. It didn't threaten me in the relationship because it was such a non-relationship at that point. Anyway I felt I would be setting myself up for a bad situation if I stayed for Christmas. I would have all sorts of expectations of real closeness, and it wasn't going to happen — I wasn't going to get anything... anything more than the physical closeness that we'd had for four months already. And I felt the frustration would be so great that I didn't want to do it, so I left. It was really just a freak thing that my brother called me and said, "I'm going to Atlanta to spend Christmas with our sister — do you want to go?" And that was important to me, but had things been different with Robert, I think I would have probably chosen Robert.

Had he been planning to spend Christmas Day with you?

Yeah.

Was this the first time he hadn't spent Christmas with his family?

Uh-huh.

And you still thought it wouldn't work and therefore would be better to avoid?

Hmmm... It was too dangerous for me. I had already felt too much isolation from him. I suppose if he had broken down and said to me, "It's so important to me for you to be here," I would have dropped everything and stayed. But he pretended that it was just — "Oh, okay."

How did he react when you came back?

Well, when I came back was real bad too. I called him on Christmas Day... 'cause the whole time I was away I really thought about him.... I had thought a lot... trying to figure out what I wanted from him, why I wasn't getting it. At least what I wanted so I could tell him. I just desperately wanted to get out of this state where I felt all closed up. And he didn't know how I felt, and I didn't know how he felt. And I thought that was horrible. It was really unbearable to me. So I called him on Christmas Day, and he said, "Okay, call me as soon as you get back and come over." So I went over there and (pause) I was really horny because I had been away for four days. And that was literally the first four days I had been out of Manhattan in over a year. And I had been out of touch with sex....

For four days....

Yeah.

Some people may find that strange.

Well, I am not saying it as though it's strange. I really wanted sex — and much more with him than anybody else. I wanted to have sex a lot, but I wanted to have it a lot more with him than with anybody else.

So what happened?

He was not into it, and also his cock was too sore from something else — I guess this other lover he had at the time, or this other boyfriend — and I felt horrible about that. I felt absolutely awful. Eh... (long pause) because I wish — I *wish* he hadn't asked me to come over that night, or I *wish* that I had gotten up and left when he told me that. But I didn't. I stayed and I felt horrible. It worked out the worst possible way it could have. 'Cause this horrible feeling drifted over me and I stayed anyway.

That's probably when I started to really pull back. I finally decided, "This is *not* worth it to me. I'm far too involved already." And... at a certain point soon after that I made certain declarations to him, like, "If you don't show some interest in me..." I guess I didn't call him for a couple of days, and he finally called me and said, "Is something wrong? I haven't heard from you." And I said, "Yeah, something's wrong. If you don't hear from me, I don't hear from you. That's something real wrong. And I'm going to stop trying to see you all the time." So I guess that's the way January went. I was really trying as hard as I could just to pull away from him.

What was his reaction?

His reaction was, "Give me time." That's what he kept saying to me: "Give me time. I know there's something here that's very important to me, but I'm very young emotionally. I can't express my feelings. Just give me time." And finally I said to him, "Okay, I'll give you as much time as I possibly can. I'll set it up so that I'm not expecting anything of you, I'll act in such a way as to *make* you come after me, to let me know that you're interested. I'll do things so that I feel comfortable, and as long as I can sustain it, that's as long as you have." 'Cause, I said, "I want to. I hope I can. You know, I hope I can give you enough time to open up to me." I remember very clearly saying that. As long as I was not going through too much pain because of it, that's as long as he had. But if it got to the point where I really felt it was get in or get out, I was going to get out. Then February came, and that's when the film script project started; and then he really didn't see me for a long time. I worked every night and every day.

You were working at the magazine during the day and at night on a script?

Uh-huh. We worked every night until two, three, four sometimes. Because we had a deadline and we were really pushing it. God, I was only sleeping two hours a day. My work at the magazine was so inane that I could do it as long as I could keep my eyes open — and I did. I never fell asleep there. And Ray would coke me up as soon as I got there every night. So that kept me awake. And then I was tricking like crazy, because I would be all coked up at two and three in the morning. It was a weird time. It was February, it was freezing, the weather was awful, and yet I would be so wired up that I would leave Ray's and walk down Broadway and always meet somebody, or go to the bars if it wasn't too late, but it was usually too late. So it was always somebody on the street. During that period there must have been like one almost every night.

I hardly saw Robert at all during that time. On weekends I guess I saw him, because Ray and I didn't work seven days a week — I think only six during that time. And Robert did say at one point that he resented it and missed me. I think he said it nastily over the phone, something like, "Well, am I ever going to get to see you?" And I said, "Well, do you ever want to? Are you ever going to make a big enough effort to see me?" And I remember by Valentine's Day I had pretty much built up walls again. So much so that I was able to go to Studio, know he was there, and not look for him.

Studio on Valentine's Day must have been quite an... elaborate presentation.

I don't remember. I think I took a purple and fell down the stairs on the balcony. I don't remember. But I was on a lot of drugs that night. Good drugs though, not shitty drugs. I was on cocaine and a purple, which for the record is a Lotus 8. It's a hypnotic, not a barbiturate. It has some of the effects of a Quaalude — makes you feel like you're drunk without having a drink.

So you got there and didn't look for Robert?

No. Actually I was hoping not to run into him. But he came up behind me at a certain point and put his arms around me — and my first reaction was " Oh no, this is *not* what I want." I had kind of decided that night I didn't want to run into him. I guess I was trying to say to myself that I was going to start getting out of it. But he swept me off my feet, which was not difficult because I was so stoned on this down and had fallen down the stairs anyway once. And I remember him just taking me off to Brooklyn. And that I was not resisting. Um... so it's funny—

Was he more aggressive than usual?

Yeah. I guess by that time my absence had built up a certain aggression in him. But if I hadn't run into him, I wouldn't have looked for him. I think things would have been different if he had not come up behind me and acted the way he did. I'm sure of it. The fact that when he first found me, I felt like I wished he hadn't, makes me feel that I was really ready to leave him. But he did find me, and he did act that way, and I didn't leave him.

How did you feel the next day?

I felt great. We had great sex, and I think I slept until very late and went into work late. (Long pause) After that sex started getting more intense with Robert.

What had been your sexual history? You started out being very "democratic," that is. . . .

With Robert, yeah.

It was a fairly easy role-reversal situation?

Yeah. I think he didn't know anything else, really. That's the feeling I got when I first met him. I mean this is the way everybody starts out having sex, in a reciprocal sort of way. And then people decide what they like better; they assert themselves in whatever active or passive way, and I have been sexually, erotically, inclined to dominant/submissive situations. Submissive is not quite the right word. Dominant is definitely the right word. Whoever I'm involved with, that's what I want from them. I want their dominance. . . . Um. . . so what was your question?

So sex was heating up between you and Robert.

Yeah. I don't remember if he was beginning to fuck me or not. I don't remember when that really started. It could have been around that time. But anyway, he was getting more into a dominant role, beginning to enjoy it. Really beginning to enjoy standing there and having his cock sucked by someone, namely me, on their knees. Lots of that. I don't remember much fucking. But I definitely saw that his sexuality was going that way. And I didn't hesitate to help him grow along those lines. . . . I did choreograph our sexuality in that way to a large extent. Because he still doesn't like to really assert himself in what he wants. And it's mainly left up to me.

So then. . . .

Okay. In March he's moving out of his apartment, looking for another apartment — calls me and asks me out to lunch. This was when *he* was beginning to court *me*. *He* was beginning to have time because he was working fewer hours, five instead of seven hours a day, and he was spending the other time doing his design job and looking for an apartment. So he would come to meet me instead of me going to see him. And that felt good. I liked that. I felt a balance was finally beginning to be struck here. So he called me, and we went to lunch, and he said, "I have something to ask you." And he asked me to move in with him. And I felt really touched.

Were you surprised?

Mmmmmm. I'm not sure. I was... I don't think I was surprised because I think I had figured it out, if only minutes beforehand. But it wasn't what I wanted to be asked at that moment. (Laughs) I was surprised that I would have to make such a decision. I was very cautious — God, real cautious. I said, "Are you sure you know what you're talking about? Are you sure you know what you want?" Ummm... And in the end I said, "No, I can't do this right now. I'm not ready for it."

Why?

Because I felt I couldn't deal yet with living with him. I felt I could deal with him as a lover whom I didn't live with, but I felt if we lived together, I would be forced to face so many things that I fear and I wasn't ready for that. I would be forced to face my feeling of inadequacy as a faggot, feelings of inadequacies, perhaps, as a man — I don't know if that's true or not. Definitely as a faggot. Perhaps as a man, I don't know. I would be forced to face the fact that I can be a jealous person sometimes. I don't like that in myself. I feel awful about myself when I feel jealousy. I felt that it would separate us, wouldn't be good for us. I feared it would end us completely, because I was sure that I wouldn't be able to do it — and I was pretty sure that he wouldn't be able to do it yet, either.

How did he react to your turning him down?

Very well, on the face of it. He gave me indications that he felt bad, but he accepted it like he accepts everything, which is very easily.

(Pause) I also padded it a lot by saying, "No, I can't do it now; let's wait and see. I think it's better if we live close to each other but in different apartments." ...Basically I was saying, "I'm just afraid, I can't face all those things you have to face when you live with someone." Especially him. 'Cause he is more uh... your typical gay man than anyone I've ever been involved with. He's less an alien, less a freak, he feels more comfortable with all the people who I feel less comfortable with. So I was aware that I was dealing with the question of living with — in certain ways — one of those faggots who always made me feel inadequate, who always made me feel like I wasn't doing something they were doing and I wasn't feeling something they were feeling. And I was afraid of that. You know, there's always been this duality with me — I've expressed myself in very extreme ways as a gay man and yet been totally alien to gay male society, which feels a lot like high school, where I never fit in. But I always thought *that* was because I was a fag. It's odd to find years later that I have the exact same feeling of not fitting into the gay world... the only difference is that in high school I could not act it. In the gay world I have gotten the whole trip down, but it still doesn't feel right.

That's an interesting difference.

You know, in high school I did stand out like a sore thumb. In the faggot world I can pull it together and—

Pass for gay?

Yeah. But I still ain't. (Pause) And in many ways he is. There's a huge cultural gap between us. It's different for me than it is for him because he can look at me and not identify himself with any of the things that I am. Whereas I have this problem of identifying myself as gay and yet not feeling a part of it. You know, he may not feel a part of many things I am, but he's never aspired to be them either. Whereas I have tried so hard to be a faggot (laughs) and can't do it. And only now am I beginning to accept that. I can't do it. I won't do it. I don't have to do it.

Which is odd, because from the outside you certainly look like a classic gay person.

Well, part of it is this chameleon sort of ability I have. I can move smoothly through very different social situations. I've worked on that ability, but it still doesn't make me feel any less like a total outsider when I stand in a gay bar. (Pause) And I'm really sort of convinced now that the trick is just accepting that. And I think I know now that Robert doesn't. I think I felt sometimes... (long pause) like I should be a faggot for him....

Getting back to Robert's moving to Sixty-third Street....

I thought that apartment and that neighborhood were dreadful, awful, but I also thought that he was making a very definite statement in his life.

Moving into a place worse than Hell's Kitchen was a statement of some sort for Robert?

Yeah... and I was impressed. I thought it was important in his development. I told him what I thought of the neighborhood, of course, which was: it's very, very, very bad. But he was making this headstrong decision and at that point I felt that it was not up to me to change his mind. So I did everything I could to support him, to give him confidence. But I was worried every second he was in that apartment. Really, seriously worried.

So then he moved in and got robbed....

Seconds later (laughs) — within *one* day actually. I think he spent one night there, and the next morning he went out to do something and got robbed, and called me. And that started a whole emergency evacuation because my feeling was just to get him out of there. This was much more than being robbed.... I know dangerous junkies when I meet them. And I met them. When I was moving his stuff in, I met these people in the hallway. This was a death trap! And yet I still felt that if he was making a decision to make a go of it, I would only support him. Which may have been wrong. Maybe I should have just said, "You fucking asshole, what are you doing here? You can't possibly live here."

Well, Hell's Kitchen is not enormously safe either, is it?

It's the building. I mean in this building — this is not exaggeration —

the junkies are there in the hallway every time you go in and out. You have to step over them. There is no security. He was the only white person in any of those buildings. He does not look as streety as I do. He cannot pass through third world environments without being noticed. I can. I don't anyway, because it's very dangerous. Even for me, it would have been out of the question to move in there. But for me the odds would have been better. You know, at a certain point I felt for sure he was going to be killed by one of these people, because it doesn't make any difference to junkies to kill someone. So I did feel that it was an emergency and that he had to be evacuated and gotten out of there immediately. So Patti and I and the dogs went over and moved him out, and into our place.

So when Robert moved in with you, it was basically an emergency measure?

Yeah. And my feeing was simply to do it — he was a mess then, he was really a mess. He was so afraid and terribly insecure, ready to get fired or leave his job. Ummm... and I felt like by that time we were good friends. I would have done this for any good friend. I just wanted to put a roof over his head, I wanted to put food in his stomach, and I wanted to comfort him. I was very nervous about him moving in to our apartment, because I was aware of the under-lying problems he and Patti would have. I thought she would handle them differently. But I was aware they were there. That made me nervous.

Also, he's allergic to cats, and you had five or six cats.

Somehow the allergies went away. Unless he handled the cats, he was no longer allergic to them. He was allergic to my house, for all that time. He was not allergic to the cats directly. He was allergic to that environment. That was a physical manifestation of hating the environment, and... I was also aware of many of the values he had and I was afraid of those. I was afraid of his neatness thing. I was afraid of the how-can-you-live-like-this? value structure he was carrying around with him. I did feel very strongly that he should put that in storage when he moved into our apartment. Because that's the way things worked there, and that's the way things went smoothly, and that's what she and I wanted from each other — the smoothness. So I was afraid of those things. And I was right. They all came up, they all got in the way.

I was also afraid of having him live with me. Not that I ever brought anyone home to that apartment — I never could bring anyone home with all those animals anyway, it had nothing to do with that. And it didn't really have to do with my being curtailed in any way, like I couldn't go out or I couldn't have tricks, because I could. He never tried to stop me from doing anything like that. I guess I was more afraid that when I had him there I would be much happier with him than going out. And I was afraid to accept that. Yes, it did mean something to me to live with him.

Well, how was living with him actually once it started?

Easy. He's easy to live with. Most of the problems that have come up since I've lived with him have been my problems. You know, they've been magnified because I live with him, because I have this gay man living with me, I have this man living with me. The largest problems I've encountered are the feelings of alienation, of being very different. That's been the biggest threat. And to work out things sexually has been a very big challenge. Because sex is terribly, terribly important to me. And it is my major source of pleasure. I think the three major points of discomfort to me were the fact that I had to face a man, a gay man, and my own sexuality in a very honest way, if he lived with me.

What do you mean your own sexuality?

Well, ummm . . . my sexual appetite for one thing. I had to figure out what sex meant between us. And it's threatening to have to figure out the intricacies of your greatest source of pleasure.

Did you become any clearer about what sex meant between you?

Somewhat. Not too clear, yet. Because I haven't figured out what it means to me yet. It's such a powerful force in my life. Such a motivating force. And it's something I seem to want all the time. It's very, very important to me. And when you have a lover with you, then all those lines have to be crossed at a certain point.

When did you start using the category *lover*?

I guess probably when he proposed to me, asked me to live with him, that's when I felt like I could call him my lover.

Did sex change when he was living with you?

Yes, sex had started changing... well, a little before that. Ummm... we became much more defined in roles. He in a dominant role, me in a... the word *passive* is not at all the right word — I'm actually extremely aggressive about it. It's a curious assertiveness. It's almost like being the manipulator of the dominant. I've always been in that position — I've always been on the bottom. So I've always wondered am I the same as men who are on top? You know, am I as much a man as they are? I've always been a little insecure about that. That's what I mean when I say that Robert as a man is difficult for me to deal with. Robert as a gay man is difficult for me to deal with — simply on a level of manhood. I haven't yet totally accepted and gotten behind my own manhood in that way. Because I've never been forced to. I've never been in a situation where the role was so transparent, where I could see through the role to the person so easily and so clearly... uhm.... Because the role falls apart in front of the person with Robert, the role I sustained with everybody else — with Jay, with Timothy....

Would you consider yourself the dominant personality in the relationship?

In certain ways, in certain ways I'm not. In some ways he's stronger than I am. I mean that's been apparent to me since he expressed this wish to move in with me. It was against my better judgment at the time, but I suspected my better judgment was worse somehow; I suspected I was afraid of things I should not be afraid of... and that's why I've gone through with this. I don't see any reason why I should be afraid of him as a man, as a gay man. I don't see any reason I should be insecure about those things anymore... I'm ready to face them. And ready to accept who I am and get behind it and feel good about it.

So what was happening with the relationship when you began living together?

Well, for a while I was working for the magazine, and then it was just very day-to-day. I would come home at five-thirty, six; I would be miserable and tired because I hated the job. But then I quit and started working with Ray, and that was working nights. So we weren't seeing each other much. We were seeing each other during the day, but he was going out at night. And I wasn't bothering to come home because I knew he wouldn't be there. And I usually wanted sex, and if he wasn't there — I mean I always felt like, Yes, I need sex, I'd rather have it with him than anybody else... but if I can't get it with him, I'll get it with somebody else. (Long pause)

Was it bothering you that he was out presumably getting sex himself?

It did and it didn't. In the logical way of thinking, of course it didn't... couldn't. But right down there, in the emotional pit of things, yes, it did. Because I'm insecure about certain things. I'm insecure when he's out there with faggots because I'm not a faggot, and I can't compete with faggots. Whatever they give him, I can't give him... and that makes me feel afraid... makes me feel insecure... makes me feel (long pause) not at ease about that. This is only something I've figured out lately, in the past couple of weeks... but I really don't feel I can compete with the rest of them. Like he's out there having these experiences, that don't have anything at all to do with me... and that makes me nervous. And it feels painful sometimes. On the other hand, I am having experiences, but they do have to do with him. They have to do with the lack of him. If he were there, I don't think I'd choose to have sex with anybody else because our sex is much better than I get from anybody else. But most of the time my sexual activity is not unrelated to him — it's related to him because he's not there. I'm having it with others because I can't have it with him.

And that brings up the whole question of sex object. Which was a real clunker when he said that to me... because Jay said it too. And — you know — I felt real guilty. Yes, I have used him as a sex object sometimes. But I have never used anybody without being aware of who they are... and especially not him. I have never lost sight of him. I've never been that selfish. And actually I think I *should* be able to use him as a sex object in that way, because I think all the other stuff is already taken care of. I do care for him as a person first. I will never lose that. I will never be unaware of his needs — personal or sexual — and only aware of my own. I'm not made like that. If anything, I have a history of being too much the opposite... that's really not a problem.

The Florence Nightingale syndrome?

Yes. So when I am a little bit selfish, it doesn't run the risk of getting into total selfishness. Now I think he said it out of insecurity — because I think he was feeling like he wasn't providing me with much of anything else... and that's a whole 'nother question.

Getting back to the relationship....

Before I went to California — to finish the final draft of the film script with Ray in Palm Springs — I was working nights, so we didn't see a lot of each other. We saw each other in the day. We had whatever sex we had in the day... and we were pretty active sexually then. Umm... we did have a problem the week before I went to California. I was really trying to muster things so I had as much time as possible to spend with him. And then he went out one night. He said he went out to go dancing, and I had no reason not to believe him. I didn't even think further about it. The point was that I was desparate to spend time with him, and he was desperate to get away from me. And that was a bad situation.

How did you feel about going away and leaving him?

I didn't want to do it at all. I really didn't.... Sure, I was excited but I was excited about finishing the work. I was also a little bit nervous. I didn't know what it was going to be like — but I knew that Ray and I would get along perfectly, as we did. And I knew that the time in L.A. would be boring, as it was. It was dreadful there. And in Palm Springs I was just isolated. For me Palm Springs was a combination of hell and paradise.

Why hell?

Because I was alone without Robert and I wanted him very much. I had to go to sleep alone every morning. I had no sex at all for three weeks. That was an enormous amount of time for me to not have sex. And by that time Bill was there. He and Ray were fucking like bunnies. There was this sex in the air, but there was none for me. So it was very frustrating sexually. And emotionally I missed him terribly. I was also going bananas because I knew things were blowing up at home. I knew that my little house was never going to be the same — and that there were forces at work that I just could not control. Even had I been there I couldn't have controlled them, but I was in a very helpless situation, three thousand miles away getting these telephone reports. And I had never asked Ray if Robert could come there; I had never discussed it with him because I really didn't know whether or not it would be too distracting for me. I was afraid it might be. But then I realized I was more distracted by fantasies and by this frustration — you know I was having sexual fantasies when I shouldn't have been — while we were working — if we were going through something particularly tedious I was having sexual fantasies.

And at the same time I was in paradise. I was in an environment where it was so incredibly beautiful physically, and the wealth of wildlife — you know, being able to just go out and look at the sky and pick out hawks and owls, and the reptiles all over the place. That was wonderful for me. It was also challenging to be alone for that period of time, and I felt good because I was weathering all this.

I felt a sense of accomplishment about that — the fact that I could be separated from him and yet not fall apart, the fact that things at home were falling apart, and I could still concentrate on my work, and that I could enjoy myself because of these things that were personal to me, this connection with wildlife that's been there always — as long as I can remember being alive I've connected to that. But as soon as I was given the option, I decided to have him come because I really wanted his companionship.

What was it like with him there?

When he came, I picked him up at the airport, and it was really moving for both of us. I was just happy to have him there. It felt wonderful to feel his body again, to smell it, to be real close to it again. For the first week he was there, we still worked, he was terrific.

Did Robert share your passion for animals and wildlife?

Yeah. Because he understands beauty, he understands the beauty of nature, he understands the colors. He's fascinated by little critters that run along the ground and strange birds that fly — not in the way I am, but, yeah, that was one of the first things that we got to really share together. We had shared some of my taste in other things like theater; I had taken him a couple of times to see way-out types of theater and some of it he liked a lot, particularly gay things I had exposed him to. But the natural beauty of Palm Springs was something we were able to share fully — and that was important, I think, in bringing us together. It was probably the thing we shared the most fully yet. As I said, he didn't have the same fanatical fascination I have with these things, but certainly he understood the beauty of them — the hummingbirds around the house, all those things. And I was excited to be able to give him this, to be able to bring him to such a beautiful place. The mountains would turn pink at sunset and sunrise, and they would go through these incredible gradations of color in only minutes.

What was the house like?

It was a very small simple house. A living room, a dining area, small kitchen, and two small bedrooms. With a swimming pool.

Not Hell's Kitchen.

Oh, please, no. It was an utter luxury. A small house, but totally comfortable. The kitchen had everything. The house was air-conditioned; the pool was outside. The town of Palm Springs itself is, you know, a very rich town, designed for comfort. Clean — the poor people you don't see, because they live too far away to be able to afford gas to get there. And in this house everything is taken care of. If something breaks, you call somebody and they're there in a second. It was luxury beyond anything either of us had.

Did you enjoy this?

Absolutely . . . and it made me appreciate certain of his values more. Actually those values I had not ever really not appreciated. I just had to put them in a different place in New York because they were not available to me or to him. I mean I had not depreciated them. I had not run them down in any way. They just didn't work here. There, yes, they worked. And he was very helpful, very sensitive while we were working. We would have a wonderful meal every day — Ray and I would pull it together and cook a meal. Robert knows nothing about the kitchen. And also I got to play wife, which is one of the things I love to do most. I don't take it seriously anymore as a lifestyle, but there it was perfect. I had the license and freedom and I knew it. I knew that this was paradise — the place for little games like this. And we played them. We really played them out.

What was Robert's reaction to your work?

Always confident... always totally supportive.

Was that important?

I don't really think so. Hmmm... I don't know though, because I never had a lack of it. I guess if he had not been supportive or not been confident, it would have been a huge problem for me. But I never had to face that because he's always been wonderful in that way and always made me feel important and talented and accomplished.

He went into our bedroom to read the screenplay when it was finished, and I could hear him laughing — that was real important, because no one was standing over his shoulder. He didn't have to laugh... he didn't have to react in any way. He reacts to things very honestly, very quickly. He also helped us very much. He did the diagrams that were in there... he drafted them... he proofread, pointing out obvious fuck-ups that we had all overlooked, and he also questioned some very questionable things.

What's your attitude towards Robert's work?

I don't understand a lot about design. I love his sense of color and anything he's done I've been very impressed with. I'm — I'm very respectful of his work. I think he does it very well. Although I myself don't have a very critical eye about it, becasue it's never been anything I've studied or looked at closely. (Long pause) Ummm... I don't know how to really judge it?

Do you think what he does is worthwhile?

Yeah... all jokes about design queens aside. First of all, I admire his skill — you know, his simple ability at drafting, to do calculations, to do all sorts of stuff like that. I have great admiration for that. And I think he's creative and practical at the same time and I have a lot of admiration for that.

You know, I don't make comparisons about our work. I'm real careful not to do that. I 've always had respect for his work. I've never been terribly involved in it because he's never gotten me involved in it. He's never wanted my opinion, or anything else really. But I've pushed him.... I'd get him work any time I could. I'll always recommend him to anybody, for that kind of work. And I would never feel uncomfortable about it. I would always feel perfectly secure, because I really do think he's good.

Was the time together in California important to you?

Something happened there so that I was able to give in to passion and romance in a way I hadn't since Timothy — which was seven years ago. Before Robert came to California, I just thought of him with madness, burning madness and passion and desire, and when he got there it didn't change. Every second I wasn't working I was glued to him. And... all the time I wasn't working, it was about pleasing him, it was about being close to him. And I got incredible pleasure out of it. 'Cause it was safe for me there, we were in a dream house. We were in paradise. So it was that whole thing of giving myself up totally to him, making myself a slave of love, which to me is a very exciting thing. But not to be done carelessly and not to be done in the wrong situation. I was able to free something in myself... I had opened the locked door to that passion. A door I had slammed and locked after Timothy. (Long pause) The feeling I had for Robert when I was in California came as close to that passion as I expect to come. It really got to the point where I could just throw myself into it without being afraid of being eaten up or crushed by it or in any way annihilated because I was just giving in, surrendering myself to a feeling. (Long pause) So when the others left us for almost a week in that little house, it was dreamy... real dreamy.

The perfect honeymoon.

Yup. Really was. And we were able to play the fantasies, the roles — I'm still not clear on how much of a part he had in it, because we did have a problem once. We only had twenty minutes before dinner, and he really wanted to fuck me, so he did, and I didn't come. And that night we were going out to dinner and then bar hopping in nearby Cathedral City. I knew that he was going to be too tired when we got home — because he always is. So I knew I wasn't going to come that night. At least not with him — it would have to be jerking off, and I hated that. But I took a walk and I sort of thrashed it out with myself, and I came to the conclusion that I should have come. I should know the importance of that to myself and I should have seen to it myself. So ultimately I didn't blame him; I blamed me. But I couldn't talk to him about it. I couldn't get the words past my tongue. . . the whole night. So I was cool and distant, I let him sleep, and I stayed angry until the next morning. And then we had a discussion about it in the morning while I was swimming around angrily in the pool, and he more or less told me that I had made all the decisions about where our sex was going. I was real upset about that because I didn't want that. That was not what I had set out to do. And also my ego was hurt. I don't want somebody doing things to please me; if they're not really into it, then ultimately I'm not going to get what I want out of them anyway. You know what I ultimately want is somebody to be able to use me to enjoy their passion, in the same way I use them to enjoy mine. So that was the first time that was ever spoken about it.

That was one of the only real conflicts — I guess the only real heavy one we had in California, aside from the heaviness of indulging in the romance of it all.

How do you feel now about getting a new apartment with Robert and moving in together?

I'm nervous about all the unresolved things — because we can't live a monogamous life. And to have to forge a new way is very frightening to me, because I find it real painful to deal with his sexuality when it doesn't relate to me.

Does he find it painful when you trick?

I don't know. I don't think so.

But you find it painful when he tricks?

Uh-huh.

Why?

Because, as I said, it doesn't relate to me — it doesn't include me or involve me in any way.

I would think that would be a reason for security.

Possibly. But I don't feel okay about it at all. I think there's a problem with me. And that's why I don't feel okay about it. Maybe I'll come to the conclusion that... um... that the problem is not with me — the problem is with *it*. You know, with the relationship that has no structure yet. That we have to come up with a structure for it.

What does Robert mean to you right now?

(Long pause) Well...

What does he mean to your life now?

(Another long pause) Well, a lot of confusion. (Laughs) He means a good friend, first, I think. 'Cause that's the one thing I'm secure about — totally secure?

Was that a question mark?

Yeah, the way I said it it was. Uh-huh. So I guess I'm not totally secure. But I'm certainly more secure with that than anything else. 'Cause when it comes right down to it, we are very decent to each other. We never do things to hurt each other. We always work those impulses out in another way and end up talking about it — we don't pull numbers on each other at all, ever. We have a real good record about that... we act very honestly in that way. I feel like at this time in my life I do want very much to live with someone. And I feel he's the best one I've ever met for me to live with. When everything is weighed, he's always come out innocent... you know....

Odd way of putting it.

Yes, because I feel when I'm in a relationship like this, that there are crimes committed against me. And that's not so. No one is committing a crime against me. Because that's what pain feels like to me — in here — the kind of pain that I feel when I know he's involved with someone else, even if it's just a trick. (Pause) So I understand it, in that way. And I can't justify giving up the good things he gives me because I have that pain. You know, he gives me warmth, which is the basic thing we started off with. And he gives me effort — a lot of effort. He really tries to understand me. And I really try to understand him. I think we're still far apart now. But I think we've gotten somewhere. And... I don't know. That's the hardest question you've asked.

What does Robert mean to me? Confusion. Because it's a mixture of magic and a certain amount of good reality, and a certain amount of vast difference. There's something magical — that's for sure. Sex with him is like sex with no one else, because there's something magical, something closer, more intimate... I suppose that's where I go off into romance. You know, I think of it as a little gift, a little cloud that falls on two people sometimes. It's just a certain clicking. And maybe that has to do with the passion from years ago... maybe it's a refinement of that. And... then there's the friendship. And then there's the vast differences, which are very challenging and very frightening at the same time.

Another way of putting that question is—

I still haven't answered it?

Partially you have. But I want to ask it in another way. You describe your relationship in words — boyfriend, lovers, "proposed to me," "marriage," — used with a heavy overlay of irony, because they're traditional words for straight relationships, and to use them is slightly campy. What does Robert mean in that sense? What does it feel like? Does it feel like a brother? A friend? Does it feel like two children playing together? Does it feel like comrades? Does it feel like a wife or husband?

A lot of those things you just said. Definitely like brothers. Definitely like a husband. Definitely like kids playing together. All those fit at different times I think. It's curious. We don't have any solid images yet. And we don't have words either.

So we borrow them.

Which is not the best thing to do. But yeah, the borrowing works, because those are images that I have, and those are feelings that I've had. There's a certain camaraderie when we're both sitting in the house doing our own separate work. There was a brotherhood when we were traveling together... the wonderment at new things we were both seeing and experiencing. This is definitely the closest male bond I've ever had. And yes, a husband — without any jokes. I have that image too. Which is a scary one to admit. You know, I feel on shaky ground. But I have to admit it because I know I'm not shaky... so it's got to be okay in whatever way I use it. But referring to straight marriage — referring to that structure — gives me the creeps. I have to honestly admit that I do, but it's really the whole point of this.

What is?

That this relationship is not going to be based on that — not going to be an imitation of a straight relationship.

Then it's going to be something that you invent for yourselves?

Either we do, or it will not succeed.

But it's a quite startling idea that you will have to invent it. Isn't it a very hard task to *invent* a new form of relationship?

I find it hard. Real hard. And that's why I'm nervous about doing it. Because I don't underestimate the difficulties.

On the other hand, you're doing it.

Yeah. I have a history of doing things in the most difficult way. Sometimes that's worked, and sometimes it hasn't.

The Liberated Don Juan and the Cypriot Beauty

I met Mark and Danae in their spacious apartment — the type built so solidly for the comfortably bourgeois in the prosperous twenties — in Hyde Park, a quiet tree-lined academic community dominated by the beautiful gothic buildings of the University of Chicago and surrounded by black ghettos and Lake Michigan. Their place is an amalgam of styles, dominated by books, plants, good reproductions, an almost oriental profusion of color everywhere and a superb sound system. Mark is quiet, somewhat reserved, good-natured and reflective; as the conversation relaxes he flashes a warm humor and a comfortable friendliness. Danae is a startlingly beautiful woman of Cypriot origin, animated by a passionate intensity and natural high spirits. She is a graduate student in her late twenties; Mark is in his mid-thirties and works for one of the TV networks as a sound engineer.

MARK

Tell me how you met Danae.

Well, I was in Hyde Park with my kids one evening and I decided to stop in Powell's Bookstore on Fifty-seventh Street, which I do two or three times a year. I walked in and first thing I noticed was this woman at the cash register, apparently the manager of the store. And she interested me almost immediately.

Do you remember your image when you first saw her?

Yeah. My first image was: here was someone unique... I didn't know why. I looked again, and she really appealed to me. I think everyone has an ideal woman, someone they may dream about or imagine, and Dan is the kind of woman I would imagine, say if I'm by myself and I'm laying in bed and I'm conjuring up an image of a woman, it would be that type of woman.

What type is that?

Well, I imagine a woman, uh, not... you know, not white, not black — someone exotic, and by that I mean dark hair, someone with... Well, let me put it this way: prior to meeting Danae, the kind of woman that turned me on would be the Sophia Loren type, not Twiggy. Not Cheryl Tiegs or the American kind of beauty, but someone like Sophia Loren — darker skin... the Latin... the

Mediterranean, yeah, the Mediterranean woman is what I think I'm turned on most by.

Danae's family comes from Cyprus?

Yeah... and I just really love her complexion and facial structure and her hair and her body. I like big women. I don't like skinny women. I don't like fat women, okay, but if they're big and substantial looking — that I like. I like big asses and big thighs, and... I could see that about her. I looked at her face and then I observed her mannerisms, and she was really quiet... and that turned me on. She was professional. She had a job; she didn't come off as being silly. I was in there ten or fifteen minutes, and from various vantage points in the bookstore, I proceeded to watch her. I didn't say anything to her. At that point I was really interested and my mind went to work — you know, how was I going to approach this situation.

You were with your kids — were you separated?

Oh, at this time I had been divorced, I guess, about two or three years.

Were you going with any other women at the time?

I was living with a woman. Yeah, as a turnaround from the old family routine, you know, with a house and the kids and going home every night. So I got out of Hyde Park and I was living downtown. But my kids live in Hyde Park and when I would take them out in the evenings, what's in Hyde Park? You have bookstores and a couple of places to eat, that's it. So I decided we'd check out a bookstore. You know, it's a very reasonable place to take kids when you have a few hours to kill.

Do you think you were consciously looking to meet someone?

No. At the time I was a little dissatisfied with the relationship I was in. It just wasn't going well. In fact, about that time I told the woman I was living with, "Uh, hey, it's about time for me to be going." And, of course, that led to a long period of negotiation. But no, I wasn't looking for another woman. It was quite accidental.

How did you decide to approach Danae?

Well. I'm aware that I can be maybe too aggressive or too clumsy, and I felt that Danae, as with most women that I would be attracted to... in that I don't, as a rule, pick up women, I mean I don't deal with women that would be easy to pick up. Okay? I don't pick up women out of bars or anything like that. I've never done that. So I felt that to approach her would be wrong. If she were the kind of woman I imagined her to be, I figured that wouldn't work. I had a rare opportunity in that she had to be there in the bookstore, so she wasn't about to leave immediately. And I had my daughter with me, who is quite gregarious and precocious, and actually helped me out. I mean you'd be surprised. . . .

How old is your daughter?

My daughter was seven at this time. This was like the third time my daughter had helped me to meet a woman. I would say, "Robin, there's a nice lady — maybe she would go to dinner." And you know, somehow she'd understand. I don't know if it's crystallized in her mind, that we are actually going to pick up a woman, but she knows I'm interested, and they kind of look out for me, the kids. So we had this little conversation in the back: I said, "Boy that's a really nice lady," and, "Hey look, we're going to eat across the street, maybe you'd like to invite her over." Robin thought about it and she handled it really well. She had a book that she was looking at and she went over and asked how much the book was, and Dan looked at her and gave an answer, and my daughter asked, "Do you go to school?" and Dan began smiling. So I knew it would work, I mean I knew that Robin would have no trouble engaging her in conversation. My son Adam is not as good as a front man, but he plays along too. They're very outgoing, they have no trouble meeting people and talking with people, especially if I'm around. So he was there too, with a book.

Anyway, Dan's remark was, "No, I'm not in school." And my daughter says, "Well my father goes to school." She says, "Oh, yeah?" "Yeah, he's like the Fonz — he goes to school at night." Which is really nice. I mean, here I am, a substantial person at night school; I've got these kids... So that's how it began... and then Dan asked a few more questions. I wasn't close enough to hear the entire conversation. I gave them a smile and kind of stayed out of the initial interaction. And, um, then I came up and I didn't address Dan; I addressed my daughter. I said maybe the nice lady would like to join us for some pizza across the street. And so Robin turns and says, "Would you come and have pizza with us?" I saw Dan hesitate — "What the hell do I do?" — I mean she couldn't really turn a little kid down. I mean what do you say to this kid? Get lost? So... she agreed.

Did you talk to her directly at all?

Yes. What I did — I was gonna give her some information, so I had to buy something. I mean I wasn't gonna go and just begin talking with her, I needed a pretext. So I bought a little book. It must have been ninety cents, and I wrote a check for it. I must have had about sixty or seventy dollars in my wallet, but I said "Please excuse me one second," and I went out to the car to get my checkbook. And, of course, she asked for my address and phone number and she wrote it on the check. We found out what time the store was closing, then we went across the street to a restaurant, and five minutes before the bookstore closed I went to make sure she wasn't gonna get away, without me finding out more that night. So I took my daughter back across the street — because it was getting dark at that time — and she went in and got Dan and brought her out. And when they came out we went across the street and had a pizza. Then I suggested that perhaps we should walk her home... now it was dark.

Did you get to talk to her?

Yes. I asked her some very general questions, like what her name was and did she live in Hyde Park, and how long she'd been here, and how long had she worked at the bookstore. I usually come to the bookstore a couple of times a year and I had never seen her. So it was more or less general information. I wanted to determine what her situation was, whether or not she was married, but I didn't ask that. I asked her other questions, and from other information I could infer that she wasn't married, and that she lived with someone like a relative. I believe she did mention a brother later on. So I had the information. I knew where she lived, even though I didn't ask her, because I walked her home. And we had a fun time, the kids and I were just playing games, trying to make a real positive kind of impression, that I'm not some kind of lumpen or derelict or. . . .

This was amazingly well planned out.

Yeah. And so I didn't ask her for any information. I didn't ask for her phone number, or where she lived. Of course, I had enough to locate her if I really needed to. So we walked her home, and I made a point of not asking her to get together again. I didn't do anything. That was the end. I had a very positive feeling from the whole experience, so I thought I did right. I just walked her home, which was two or three blocks, and we played a game. I got the kids involved in jumping over the cracks in the sidewalk and seeing who could walk along the ledge — we were just all over the place. I was trying to see if I could get her to participate, to see where she was. I saw that she could have gotten really taken into that. So we walked her to her door, and that was the end of the encounter.

So what did you do next?

I didn't do anything next. Uhhh, I thought about her, you know. I really did. And I thought about calling. I said No, I wouldn't just call the next day.

Did everything that you found out about Dan support your original feelings?

Yeah, it really did and even more so, because I was surprised to find, for instance, that she was not heavily involved with anyone, which was really very nice and somewhat surprising, because she's a very beautiful woman. I could be just hung up on my own stereotype, but—

No, she's a startlingly beautiful woman.

Right. You're just not going to find a beautiful woman that's young and healthy, out in the world and not with anyone, you know? So I knew that she was a normal kind of person; somebody has to be giving her some kind of attention. But I really didn't do anything, for a couple of reasons. One was the approach, but there was a very important constraint also, and that was I was still living with someone. Even if I wanted to, I would not have launched into a campaign of direct assault and rapidly develop a relationship, because that would have put me into a very difficult situation.

So I felt the thing to do was work more on developing a friendship, to get her hooked in that way and to play down the sexual aspects, which anybody can do. I felt that if I could ingratiate myself and show that I'm a very substantial person, that is more permanent and would have much more force in whatever happens at some future date than just going off into a heavy romantic thing.

Hmm. So what did happen?

Well, what I did is — I left it that way and I thought about calling her and I — I just pretty much vacillated, every other day or so I thought about that, and this went on for about a week. I thought that on the upcoming weekend maybe I would go by the bookstore again and go through a routine: "Hi, I'm back again and maybe we can get together, or whatever." All of that wasn't necessary, because I received a letter from her, and I was very... very pleased and happy about that. She wrote that, well, we didn't really make any plans after that night and it would be nice if we could get together, and she invited me up to her house. At that point I felt that I had a very good chance of getting over... depending upon how our next encounter went. But I had to make some time.

Again, there was some game playing on my part. I had to make some time to see her, which I did. I was able to free up like four hours, on a weekend. But I turned down coming into her house. She got me up there and offered me something to drink or something to eat, but I said no, and I pretty much insisted that we go out. I took her to a restaurant on Sixty-third Street, and we ate, we had some pleasant conversation and I determined that she's a woman with a lot of enthusiasm, really outgoing, just a basically decent kind of woman. And I took her home. I let her know that I enjoyed it very much, that I would like to see her again, and she was amenable to that, and that's where it was left. Fortunately, our schedules at that time — let's see, she was off on Monday and Tuesdays, and I was off on Sundays and Mondays, which worked out that Mondays were a day that we were both off, and we ended up getting together the following Monday. But my whole thrust at that time was to develop the friendship and downplay the romantic, sexual thing. And I think very early — what I was pushing on her was not a rejection of her, but that I really liked her a helluva lot. I mean, she did for me some things other woman didn't provide me with — and that's friendship and someone to talk with. So pretty much what we did was sit in restaurants and have a meal together and maybe sit in the park over here and we'd talk, or go to the museum — those kinds of activities. Things that happen in the day, because I didn't see her at night — no clubs or things like that, but museums and walks and parks.

Had you tried this tactic earlier on other women? Had it been successful?

Well, yeah, variations of the tactic. I mean, I look at the situation and I try to assess the situation to the woman. But by and large, I have been most successful in coming out of either an intellectual bag, an academic scene, or a work scene. That's my primary source of meeting women. I do not meet women in bars or in motels and all that. And very seldom at parties. The relationships usually begin because of some project, some mutual involvement in something. And because of that we would be friends or we would have some reason to talk and to spend time together.

What kind of work do you do?

I'm an engineer with a broadcasting network. I'm in a technical support maintenance aspect, which means I don't operate cameras and crap like that. The job I do can be done in an office and it's a nine-to-five kind of thing. I work primarily with a lot of people who work in repair equipment and install systems and modify existing systems. Responsible for the technical engineering aspect of the equipment that is being used.

What are you studying in school?

I'm studying mathematics. I got a degree in engineering about sixteen years ago, and there's been a virtual revolution in electrical engineering since then... pretty much everything has become obsolete. So right now I'm studying computer science and learning about the new digital computers and things like that.

How old are you, by the way?

I'm thirty-six.

To get back to Danae. How long did this... platonic dating continue?

I think that went on for four or five weeks, where I saw her maybe one day a week or so — before I actually kissed her or anything. But after that I really — you know I really began just wanting her, which I think served as an impetus to get this other situation resolved. I wasn't *really* comfortable in that kind of situation. And so, somewhere about that time, Dan, being fairly intelligent, wondered about — "Hey, like where do you live... and do you have a phone number that I can reach you at?" I gave her my number at work. And I gave my mother's address. I have my mail go to my mother's house because there's less of a hassle with moving, you know, fairly regularly. It was just such a pain to have your address changed, so I had my mail delivered out there and I would go out on weekends and collect it. So Dan asked, and I just told her on the phone, "Yeah, well, you know, I live with someone." And she was a little disappointed.

She was....

Well she was very disappointed. We talked for a little bit more and fortunately I had not *lied* — you know, I may have omitted some things, but I didn't *lie*... I just was not going to do that. And I presented it in a very matter of fact way — "Oh yeah, you know."

And by this time you were kissing....

Yeah, but it was... platonic kissing, it was like people who really liked each other. It wasn't really a sexual kind of kissing. I was trying to avoid that. And it was *really* difficult to be near her, because about this time I mean, shit, I'm hard, you know. So I didn't — I tried to avoid that kind of close intimate contact. But it was platonic... because I thought it would have been disastrous had I slept with her and then told her. That would have been disastrous. She'd have really been pissed behind that. And if I were going to spend some time with her after this other relationship, which I knew was on its way out, I thought she could never trust me, if I were to do something like that.

So you told her you were living with someone and you still kept seeing each other on Mondays, or did it create a change?

Yeah, there was a slight change. I think the way the conversation ended up, I said, "Look, I just enjoy so much spending time with you." As I recall I wanted to put a trip on her to the effect that, "Hey, you mean to tell me you're not going to see me anymore or talk with me. I mean I haven't violated anything, you know, simply because I live with someone. I'm still the same person you knew an hour ago." So I left it like that and I felt then that I was in a good position. And it came round. We got together the next Monday or on a weekend — I don't really remember. But I'm glad it came out. I didn't want to hide it, and so I purposely left little indicators. I wanted to be subtle and I wanted it to be very matter-of-fact and incidental, that I was living with someone. I really wanted her to know — I didn't want her to know right away — I wanted her to know after she knew me. Yeah. (Pause) And that's where it stood. And the reason is, I wanted to see if she were amenable to having the relationship develop further, given that she knew that I was living with a woman.

And?

The truth is, I had no problems with living with one woman and be dealing with her. I mean if it were possible to accommodate the situation, I could have become involved with her. I don't have any hang-ups about that. So long as I let the first lady know I was leaving and we were negotiating — she didn't want me to go — and Dan knew I was living with someone. I wouldn't have had any problems with it.

How did things develop then between you and Dan?

Well it continued — she knew what the situation was. Okay, maybe she didn't like the situation. I'm sure she didn't like the situation, but there was enough there to allow our relationship to develop. And it did. I continued to proceed very slowly, because I didn't want a rush, a real change that would indicate something radical was about to happen, like I had just fallen completely in love with her and I'm leaving my girlfriend and I just got to be with you — that kind of thing. It wasn't that way. It developed very systematically. From the day she knew I was living with someone, or maybe it was a week or two later, I began touching her and relating to her in a romantic way... you know it was not sex, but it was... I'd begin touching her back or her hair, and of course I would kiss her, and lots of hand-holding and keeping her close, putting my arm around her and all that kind of thing.

And how did she respond?

Oh, very favorably. I knew she was responding very favorably to that — she's that kind of woman. I mean if she's approached properly... being sensitive to her and just touching her and talking to her is more important, I think than actual intercourse. You can do more, I think, talking with her. And she began letting me know that. She made offers, you know, "Well, you can spend the night here if you want," and that kind of thing, which was really very hard to turn down.

And you did turn her down?

Yeah.

Why?

Well (laughter) — the woman I was with was extremely jealous. That has to be the only reason I can think of for turning her down. Nothing else.

How did you end up finally sleeping together the first time?

Well, we met once at a restaurant, and I just began talking very erotically to her. "You're just a fantastic woman — you turn me on erotically," and that kind of thing; "I just wish so much that I could touch you, but I care about you, and our friendship is so important that I'm not going to sleep with you." And I, uh, talked to her very directly in a basic kind of way, and prefaced it by saying it's really very difficult for me because I want you so much, but I'm not going to sleep with you, but I want you to know I want you and I care about you and you turn me on, and — and the whole bit. And I'd touch her. And I knew really that I could have laid her right in the car, right there on the street, up on Grand Avenue somewhere, coming out of the restaurant.

There were a couple of incidents like that, where there was verbal fucking, right? So I was in her house and I said, "Hey, look, I gotta go, you know." I had to get home, right? Anyway I ended up spending twenty minutes or a half hour at the door just holding her and kissing her — I kissed her on the mouth, on the lips, on the neck, and I was just holding her, you know. And, uh, so we went into the bedroom and she says, "Well you can come and lay down, you don't have to do anything, but just come and lay down with me, please." And I said, "Okay." She had a skirt on at that time. It was the first time I actually saw her thighs when she laid down. She had on her panties and a skirt, she was dressed. And I wanted very much to just touch her but what I did is, I began kissing her on her thighs — she layed down and I kissed her — and she was very hot. I kissed her on her thighs and I touched her ass and I played with it. I didn't take her panties off. And she was really just very, very hot and when I finally — I kissed her, with her panties on, I kissed her, she was extremely wet; you know, which really turned me on, so I just — I was just licking there and she closed her legs and had an orgasm — she just — you know, she came. And I felt it, because my mouth was there, so I just kissed her a little more for five minutes and she got very relaxed and I came up and kissed her. And she held me — she was really very satisfied, and, fuck, I was really (laughter) — I was horny but. . . .

I can imagine.

I was (laughter) I was *very* horny but I said, shit man, you know. . . .

This seduction technique takes terrific self-discipline.

It *was* terrific self-discipline. I mean it was all I could do — I just really wanted her very much — *BUT I DIDN'T*. And I finally got to my car and I said holy fuck, you asshole! But by the time I got to Twenty-second Street, with the windows rolled down, I kind of cooled down a little. But that. . . I just really thought about it. Because I actually enjoyed it even though I didn't get any physical interaction out of the whole thing. It was very nice. I mean, that told me — I enjoyed that becuase she certainly wasn't frigid and a whole bunch of other things. Yeah, so that was the first time it was anything you can call lovemaking, if you exclude holding her and kissing her and all that. That was the first time.

So how long after that before you — had reciprocal love?

I think, it was like the next time. I really had to laugh... the next time I was here — I don't know if it was like two days or four days or what — she really came out. She said something very funny, she asked me very seriously, did I have some kind of war injury? She was going to be understanding by this time — "Hey, maybe this guy hasn't got a cock or something." But no, but no, I think she must have known that just by being close, so she knew that. But yeah, I really found it kind of funny and I thought, "Oh shit, this is really silly." I thought about it and decided this should be really very nice and it was pretty much the same kind of situation: we went to the bedroom and I undressed her — and that was a *real* pleasure for me — and I undressed and got in bed with her. And I would have really liked to have spent a lot of time with her, but I only had a couple of hours, right? But it was very, very pleasurable. I never had a problem with orgasms or anything like that. As I recall, what happened was that I was playing with her and I was just getting going and then she came, and I hadn't penetrated or anything. But I really enjoyed her, I just like her skin, I like her body a lot. I was kissing her all over and just really enjoying her with my mouth, and uh — I *swear* she's the *best* tasting woman I've ever had (laughs), she's the best tasting woman. I guess there must be people made for people because I didn't enjoy making love with my wife during the time I was married. Now it very well may be that I had too many hang-ups back there. But as a rule, I really didn't engage in oral lovemaking with my wife. And I enjoy it a great deal with Dan. I enjoy the thighs — I enjoy the thighs very much in oral lovemaking, you know. I enjoy just kissing — just, what can I say? But she's my idea of — you know, that's my fantasy — I get so turned on.

So from the beginning your sex was terrific?

Oh yeah, it was. It's no problem — I'm very, very, very happy. I'm really turned on by how someone looks... uhm, I'm not turned on by what kind of car they drive and clothes and all that. I mean how the body looks and feels and of course the first thing that I see, looking at Dan, is her face. She's got full thick lips and that really turns me on. She's got these really thick lips, and they're just beautiful. I don't like thin lips. Her mouth turns me on, I can get off just looking at her mouth. and her thighs really turn me on. That's one way I fantasize seeing her, I mean if she wanted to turn me on, she could just sit down and open up her legs and just sit there and show me her thighs completely dressed — that's all that's necessary.

Would you say that your lovemaking with her was better than any of the other women that you've made love to... is it the best or what?

Yeah, it's fuller, because with the lovemaking there are so many things that I enjoy doing. Now prior to the woman that I had been living with — the woman I had lived with before that was, quite frankly, masterful. I mean she just had a tremendous amount of experience with men. I'd lived with her for seven months, and every day two or three different guys would call her. She'd say, "Hey look, I'm living with someone." It was amazing. I'd never seen anything like that. And she's done everything there is to do and things you can't imagine, okay? The point is she had a lot of techniques, and I lived with that lady seven months and I learned a lot.

She stayed with me for seven months — twice as long as any other man. You know I really believed she loved me. I mean she just said it and said it and I really believed she loved me, but she just needed other men. She was just not a monogamous person. And believe it or not, for the first time in my life, I didn't — I couldn't understand it or accept her right away, but later on I could really understand it and we still have a very good friendship. I don't see her that much, but it's still very real, and I can understand. I think I've become a little bit enlightened, and I think I can admit something like that. Believe it or not, I can.

Do you consider yourself monogamous?

You mean one person at at time?

Yeah.

Yes, I'm monogamous because — well, if I weren't, I don't think Dan would dig it. And I don't really have an objective need not to be. I look at other women, I think about it and all that. I personally would not have any problem making love to another woman, but it wouldn't be good for the relationship. And again it's the same old dual standard there. I mean, I would *not* look favorably upon a situation whereby she had other boyfriends. I just wouldn't go for that. So, am I monogamous? I guess so. I haven't felt the inclination not to be. I look, I eyeball — I think: she'd be nice or she's got a *nice* ass, that sort of thing — but actually planning or being with someone? No, I haven't.

What happened after you started having sex? You were seeing each other several times a week or...?

Yeah, you see what happened — she basically comes on; she wanted to see me more, and I just really couldn't. I really couldn't accommodate her. I was still involved with this other woman. And so we broke up.

You mean you and Dan broke up?

Right. Yeah, yeah, we broke up. I was beginning to realize that something's — I've got a problem because I just went through, very quickly, three different women — okay? And I said I've got a problem, so what I am not going to do is move in with someone. I didn't want to fall head over heels. That's the first thing. That has nothing to do with Dan; it has to do with my *own* development. After I got divorced, I was with one woman, and that just didn't work out. Then I immediately moved my clothes from this woman's house to the next woman's house. So now I said, It's about time that I get out of here and just not put myself in this kind of situation. I should really be by myself.

Had you always been with a woman since your wife?

Yes.

And how old were you when you got married?

Twenty-one. Right out of college. And prior to that I was living with my mother. So, from year one, I was *always* living with a woman. I never lived by myself, and I think that was a factor. The other factor was that I was with a woman. Those two things coupled with the fact that by this time I knew that Dan was a serious kind of woman. It wasn't some kind of game or anything like that. And I did not want at that time to get really heavily involved. So we had this breakup. Came May, I moved out and I moved into a place in Hyde Park. I had an apartment on Lake Shore Drive — a very nice apartment — up on the twenty-sixth floor. But you asked me concretely how we broke up.

I meant was it a specific argument?

It wasn't a specific argument. She wanted to spend more time together and, uh, why was I still living with this woman? So those two factors. I mean she just wasn't tolerating my living with another woman. And so there was a split. There wasn't a real argument. I did not go out and break up with this other woman and move in here with her, or leave with the idea that something like that was just going to happen within the next couple of weeks.

Dan had decided that she didn't want to see you again because she couldn't deal with it?

Yeah, well, that's what she said, but I never believed that. As I recall, it lasted ten days, then I began seeing her again.

Who called up whom?

Let's see, that time I think I called. And then we got back together. She was at the bookstore, and I went out and bought some flowers. She wasn't going to talk to me, she wasn't there, so I left her a couple of dozen flowers and a card to the effect that I'd like to see her again. And that evening when she came in, she got it. So I received a call from her, and we got back together again.

On your terms? On a limited basis?

Yeah, pretty much on the same basis that had existed before. See, it was in May, and I was making preparations to really leave the other woman's house at this time. I had taken a lease and I had a month, maybe longer, to wait before I could actually move in, which was in June. So I was just kind of waiting around at that point, buying things, because I had never had an apartment. And then I moved into my own place.

Did you enjoy setting up an apartment for the first time?

Very much. I was the best housekeeper I have ever seen. I always kept my place very together. People enjoyed coming by. It was an extremely comfortable place. And I enjoyed it a helluva lot.

Did you cook?

Yup. I cooked and I sewed — you know, everything you do. I really wanted to do this because in my mind I had to be independent and all that: it was important for me. And I kept the place really organized, never a dirty dish laying around. I enjoyed doing the shopping and taking care of things.

So you spent the summer living in your own place, seeing Dan. Were you still seeing the woman you moved out from?

Yeah. Uh... And I was seeing other women too. About this time I began seeing other women, but as friends, you know — another objective I had was to see if I could develop friendships with women, which I was really unable to do. I mean my whole orientation was always very sexist, really macho. I couldn't deal with having a woman as a friend.

What was your background? How did you grow up?

Well, it was very... it was traditional... Chicago... South Side... you know, Sixty-first and King Drive, South Parkway....

What class... working class?

Yeah, working class, just a bunch of poor folks — nine: there was nine brothers and sisters. And my mother was a staunch Catholic, a *real* staunch Catholic. That's probably why I had all those brothers and sisters. And my father was a door-to-door salesman, selling women's lingerie.

Are there many black Catholics? Is that unusual?

Yeah, it's somewhat unusual. I mean, from my perspective it seemed like there were a lot, everyone in the school seemed to be Catholic. But I guess I don't really know how many were actually church-going Catholics. It just never occurred to me to ask that. Yeah, I think it's unusual. Traditionally blacks, by and large, are Baptists, coming out of some kind of Southern tradition.

Did you grow up fairly conservative insofar as sex roles are concerned?

Yeah, like the women were chattel. Woman stays home and makes beds and cooks and stays out of the man's business. Oh, this is a real trip for me to be adjusting.

I get the impression that, in fact, you are an unusually liberated man. How did that happen?

I guess it's by getting knocked down a lot. What I had found is there are many, many women who would fall into that old role, but, boy, are they boring! I mean — I just didn't like it. I should say — and this is not answering the question directly — but I'm just amazed. No one ever told me, for instance, that you're not supposed to make love in the light, but I just believed that the only way to make love was in the dark. It was something dirty, you did it under the covers, and I'm not sure *why* you did it. It's just something that maybe you *had* to do — but we never had any sex education or anything like that.

I think that Catholics put a real trip on you; they do everything to make sex something really nasty and bad and they reinforce all the other bullshit that's imposed upon you. Just really keeping folks in the dark. And I firmly believed that if a woman wasn't a virgin, she was *no good*. I mean even to the point like, if I had a girlfriend and she wasn't a virgin, she was just diminished, like two giant steps *down the ladder*. That's not the kind of lady I would be married to, but she's-all-that-I-got-right-now kind of thing. But how I got liberated.

Well, I think in the process of re-examining my views towards the Church and my political views and a *lot* of bullshit that had been put on me, I think it followed the same process. The same process that turned me against organized religion. Although I think my sexual development was much more significant. That happened recently.

Sex was always important for me. Even when I was married, I found myself thinking about other women, and there were occasions where I masturbated, and I had a *wife*. I thought about other women, but I didn't act it out or anything. My development has really happened in the last five years, just seeing women out there, having women talk to me at the job and being out in the world. You talk to other people and see what they're doing; you hear so-and-so is having an affair. At the same time you have the women's liberation movement, along with the gay liberation movement, and there's this inundation — all the protest movements and just this awakening, right? And... that really had an impact on me. I began to think that I wasn't being fulfilled sexually. Okay? And then I also saw that the relationship I had with my wife was not totally fair. I saw that very early and I was able to encourage her to go to school and things like that, which she did. I mean, she's an attorney now. So just in trying to put *people* in some proper perspective, just in seeing all people, men, women, black, white, just in being democratic, a lot of the myth is exploded.

I did some important things during the period I was married that I felt served to liberate me. I worked in the civil rights movement and I traveled, went down in Mississippi and some other places. I was also exposed to some very progressive people at Antioch College, in the alternate educational program, the black studies program. I met people there and I saw people smoking dope and shit like that. And, yeah, I tried it — something I never told my wife at the time — she's very traditional — but you know it wasn't so bad. And I began reading things, and a real important thing was being exposed to Marxist philosophy. That just forces you to deal with things in a progressive fashion. And the way I got to that is the concrete *oppression* I experienced because I'm not white just made me think.

I was fortunate enough to meet a man who really began struggling with me. He was a Marxist and he had little black study groups. I began sitting in and listening and arguing with him, because there was just no way I was going to accept that crap, right? And in the process, it made me think and it gave me the instrument to begin ferreting out what this reality is all about. I could see that, hey, you know, with regards to this racism, this shit is wrong. I mean, I can *see* that. Because you talkin' 'bout *me*. And that was, admittedly, very difficult, and even more difficult were your gays and things like that. But I had the instrument.

I had the tools and I began using those tools to deal with some social reality. And I think that's all that was really needed for me to go ahead and deal with my own attitude towards women and sex. I just did not want a woman that would be servile. Someone that's obsequious, I just couldn't... I wouldn't have been able to deal with that. Even though it would have been nice. So... I got into looking for intelligent women. I'm just attracted to... you know, intelligent women. They won't put a real trip on me. Once I became divorced, then of course there was no stopping me.

The first woman I was involved with after my divorce was the complete antithesis of my wife. You are just not going to lay down any bullshit with her. No way, so... hey, you know, this is something that really goes against me, and I really get into hating this bitch. I mean, somebody that's fucked fifty men or whatever. You're asking *me* this? So it was kind of a love/hate thing. I knew she was intelligent and all that. We had class together, and she just intrigued the hell out of me. By the way, she was white, and I'd never been with a white woman in my whole life. Never held hands or anything like that. So in every way, she was alien or foreign — the complete antithesis of what I was used to. That was a hell of an experience. 'Cause we just... what can I say, it was just completely different. And I think after that I naturally had to see women in an altogether different light. And I did.

The next woman that I was involved with — I mean, there were women that I'd dated, but the next heavy involvement — was another extremely strong woman. Worked with the union, you know, and she intimidated many, many men. She was that strong. No bullshit. And it was the first woman I'd met that somebody said something to her, she says, "Go fuck yourself." (Laughter) Really, she could put you in your place real quick. So obviously I wasn't about to bring a lot of bullshit into that relationship. And I was able to accommodate that, make the adjustments, and I guess that's the process of being liberated. And I see that at this point I'm not going to be with someone who I can dominate.

This is not to say that I'm not going to try, because I will try and if I can't get my way, I can act real shitty. And I've had my feelings hurt. Someone like Danae just talks to me very direct: "You can't come in here and dump your shit on me. You just clean up your act, that's all." And it's good because you take that, coupled with the fact that women are here working, paying the bills. This is also good because, see, I'm relieved of a lot of crap. I'm relieved of that responsibility. Like if I got a dependent woman, then there's 100 percent burden on me. So I think it's good. I'll be happy when they pass the ERA and all that. I realize that I have problems and I'll continue struggling with my own problems, but if the women are out here, on an equal economic and social footing, then we'll get this shit cleaned up.

It's nice, because you come into the situation where women have their own places, they drive their own cars, they have their own jobs and bank accounts and all that. And it's not about, look, I meet you, get married, and — boom — we have four kids and move out to the suburbs. Those days are *over* with. I mean, can you imagine me asking a woman, are you a virgin? (Laughter)

So let's get back to the summer. You're living in your place and you and Danae were seeing each other . . .

Yeah, but the relationship is cool. We kinda got back together, but it really didn't develop from that. Danae is a very strong woman, and there were some things about her that just made me uncomfortable. I couldn't get my way with her, in arguments and some other things. And this is the first woman that has pulled some reverse chauvinism on me. Here I'm worrying about being chauvinist and domineering, and she can really come out of a box on you. So there was some apprehension on my part, like maybe I just won't be able to handle this woman. She will ask you questions very directly, like, "Why won't you sleep with me?" Or, "Are you sleeping with someone else?" Or, "Well, I just can't accept that logic."

And most of the positions she took were fair positions. For instance, one bad habit I've had all my life is to make a date and not give a firm time. I'd say, "I'll see you on Saturday." That meant I'm coming by, you just wait for me, I'll be there sometime Saturday. And she says, "Well, what time? Because I don't know if I'm going to be here." "Hey, what do you mean you don't know if you're going to be here. You're supposed to be here waiting on me and don't worry about the time. Just be here waiting on me and don't worry about the time." So once I pulled that and she just let me know, "What kind of shit is this? I've been waiting for you for two hours." My reaction was, she was right, but I had a negative reaction to the thing. She wanted to know exact times; she wanted to know exact dates. And as I sit here now, that's only fair. But at the time that's just the way I operated. (Pause) For some reason I just couldn't bring myself to give exact times and dates and commitments and all that. So it made me apprehensive. Maybe this woman is just a little too strong for me; she's nice to be friendly with, but I'm not so sure if I want to be involved with her. She just may be *too* progressive, too demanding.

I lived by myself for a year, seeing other women... I learned that women have really changed a lot and... that's just something I would have to adjust to and accept. Once I saw a woman and really got turned on, really pursued her very aggressively, and made love to her... I thought that I spent a lot of time with her and all that. I was going to go, I mean I was finished, and she says, No, she says, you're not through. Right? And that was interesting. So I quickly learned that women are people too.

So in the summer the relationship was cooling off a bit?

Yeah, right, that was at the end of the summer. Then I went to... (pause) the Iberian peninsula with the woman I had previously lived with. I suppose that as far as Danae was concerned, it was just a bit too much. I went away for a little over a month and got back in November or something like that. And I saw Danae one or two times. And she just got tired. I wasn't seeing her enough. She says, "This is bullshit. We aren't going to see each other anymore." So in October, she stopped seeing me.

How did you feel about that?

Well, I was still apprehensive. In a way I was not really crushed, because I had these reservations. It had an impact, but what could I do? I felt that by this time she was really pushing a little bit; she came off, in my opinion, a little demanding. And I'm not saying that it was unjust or they weren't legitimate complaints, but I was not amenable to those kinds of demands. And so I just said, "Look, I understand." And we very peaceably separated. Of course, I went through the routine of asking her to reconsider and all that, but at that point I was not going to get into any kind of really heavy commitments. And that's where it stood.

Did you feel confident that you would get back together?

I felt confident... maybe I didn't at that point. I mean, I wasn't absolutely convinced that I *would* see her again. But I felt confident that I didn't do anything to really hurt her, and that in one sense, she was really pushing. I hadn't really done anything to violate the understanding we had had before. I didn't break any commitments. I just didn't let go of certain other relationships and some other commitments I had. I couldn't do both things. I couldn't continue to be relatively independent and begin working out some problems I felt I had with my own personality and with women.

So you were seeing several other women in this period?

Right. I went to Spain with this one woman because she is an excellent person to travel with. She happened also to be rather demanding and extremely jealous, which was a slight drag 'cause I ran into a very nice lady I spent three days traveling with. It really couldn't develop. By that time it was clear that I was not committed to her — the woman that I was traveling with — but we had made plans to go on this trip several months before, in fact when I was still living with her. And there were other women.

So you and Danae didn't see each other for about three months?

Yeah. Until mid-December, I guess.

How did you see each other again?

Well, it was interesting. I hadn't seen her since October. It was mid-December, and I had actually begun missing her a little bit. The women I was seeing — while it was exciting, they just did not satisfy me. Some were much smarter and richer, and they each had things no other woman had, within my experience, but I thought about Dan. I enjoyed imagining what she looked like and imagining having my head on her belly and her breasts and whatnot. And one night I was home and I get a call. This is very late, as I remember it, like one or two in the morning. "Who in the hell is it?" I thought. And sure enough it was Danae. She was at some bar, and I said, "Oh, I was just thinking about you and I tried to call you a week before and I didn't get an answer." Which was true. I subsequently found out that she was at home with somebody else when I called. She said, "Can I come by?" I said, "Sure." We've been together ever since.

You didn't move in right away . . . .

No, no. She first called near the end of December. I saw her a little bit on Christmas; I think I passed on New Year's because I had some prior commitments. And in January it just really took off. I saw her on Tuesday, then on a weekend, Friday, Saturday, and Sunday. . . . It seems like just about every other night I would see her. The only exception would be if I got tied up with work or some other. . . .

Were you still seeing other women?

That would be the only time when I didn't see Danae. But I think it averaged out to be like four times a week, maybe five times a week. Yes, and I was seeing other women, but I'd really cut it down. One woman I was seeing once or twice a week, that went down very quickly to like once every two or three weeks, and another one I'd seen two or three times a week, that went down to once a week. But it settled down tò where basically I was seeing, on a regular basis, like three women.

Danae knew about the other two?

Yeah. No, well, with Danae it was four women.

Oh.

Yeah. So I was pretty active, and it tires you out. (Laughs) Course I wasn't doing anything else, other than working and going to the gym. I stayed in pretty good shape, ran five miles every day, but it got really crowded 'cause I was seeing her like four times a week and then I was seeing one twice a week and I was seeing another one maybe once a week and another one every three weeks or something like that. And sometimes it got rough on the overlaps. And I was home very, very seldom. And. . . it kind of went that way. . . and after a month or two I said I've got to phase some of this out. I was feeling a little bit better about Danae. She kind of cooled down a little bit. She was less agitated and less insecure about some things. And she became a lot of fun to be with.

What would you do? Make dinner, watch television, go to the movies?

Well, that period, we made love *a lot*. And it was a very strange thing. I mean, you're supposed to be very active when you're a teenager. I can remember being horny a lot but nothing like this. I just couldn't get enough of her. I just couldn't. And I don't really know how I did it, it was four or five nights a week until four o'clock in the morning, *many* nights, *many* mornings watching the sun come up. I just *never* got to bed before three o'clock. And it was very pleasant for me.

I guess I worked out some things. I knew that I could keep a house better than any woman I know. I could cook; I could take care of myself. And that was a big thing for me. Having a mother that was a slave, I did nothing coming up. For the first time I made my own travel plans, I didn't have to have somebody do that for me. I just completely took care of everything. There was nobody doing anything. Period. And on top of it I had money in the bank. So all of that was satisfying. Whatever needed to be dealt with was dealt with. And for the first time I wasn't attached or living with anyone — I didn't have a tit in my mouth. That was very good for me. And... as I sit here now, I don't have any problems thinking What would I do if this woman left me? That's no big deal. I'd just keep going, you know? I just don't necessarily need a wife, and I just don't necessarily have to have someone to take care of me. So I suppose that's a part of being liberated.

At this time Danae was in school?

Yeah, she had started back to school. I cooked dinner every night, not because she was in school but because no one has ever come into my house and cooked dinner. No one has ever come into my house and done anything.

And something else that happened. And this is very unique. The building I lived in had an inordinate number of single women — I guess because it had a doorman and was very safe. So there's a woman down the hall, two women down the hall. There's an Afro-Korean woman, *beautiful* woman, model, whom I met. So just in the building alone I quickly became friends with four women. And my first lover lived in the other building. Little old, foxy old woman that had married twice and was now divorced, she lived in the other building. So, man, there were lots and lots of women. In addition to that I had three women that really dug me. I had a policy: I just was not going to sleep with any woman in the building. But what I did get into is, I got into a situation where the women would come by and rap to me. At one time, I had like seven women in my crib, right, just rapping. We had a party and I was the only man. And we'd talk about men and about how bullshit they are, how they have so many problems. So I felt good getting off into that, and in addition to the women I was having sex with, I was sleeping with these women for the first time, all of them. But I wasn't fucking them. If you can imagine that.

You were sleeping with them, but without sex?

Yeah, right. I mean...

You mean the ones in the building?

Yes, right, right, and you know—

That's odd.

Right. It was odd. But I got some pleasure, because... like one, Sandy, she had the nicest breasts, huge, beautiful breasts. She was very attractive, very nice, a black woman, intelligent. And she'd come on by, and so it got around that I was okay. I mean I didn't go around trying to knock over everything in sight; I had a very good reputation.

They would stay and sleep the night but you wouldn't have sex?

Yeah.

Is that common amongst straights?

Hell, no. No, no, no, it's not common — it's not common with *me*.

I never heard of that.

Okay, but you have to understand the situation. First of all, I was making love five times a week, going to the gym and all that. I really felt very good about myself and I had a *choice*, okay? And I guess I was trying to construct the possibility of dealing with maybe ten or twelve women. I could have slept with any one of the ten women if I really wanted to. But I just didn't have a need to — to fuck just to prove something. There's a woman I work with and she still lives here — she was a young thing, what a beautiful ass, just really a sweet woman, you know, just sweet and black and full of life. And I spent time with her. The relationship developed because of our juxtaposition at work, where I rapped with her every day. So she ended up coming by, and it was interesting, because one day she says, "Oh, can I take a shower?" And she was relatively shy. I guess it just got down to a point that maybe she thought I was shy or something. And it occurred to me, well I had better tell her that I'm not going to sleep with her.

But anyway... yeah, they come by and — but don't get me wrong; I would have erections, okay? It was just an active, conscious decision not to fuck. I mean I would want to — yeah, I would want to fuck; if I could do it and not suffer the repercussions, I would have done it. Just like now, okay? You know, Dan satisfies me and all that, but you asked me, what would happen if I fucked this woman? If I knew no one would ever know and all that? Sure. A one shot deal kind of thing, yeah. So to answer your question, no, I don't think it's common at all because most straight men are married, aren't they? Maybe it's changed today, but I mean they're in some way really hooked into something and they're into that traditional monogamy thing — either that or they're off trying to screw everybody that walks.

How did Dan deal with the fact that you were surrounded by so many women?

She was there and she saw what the situation was and because of my behavior and what other people were saying, there was just no question. I can't imagine her being uncomfortable. I don't know what she could have done about it anyway. But she saw who the women were, and I think she felt confident. I mean, if you look at Dan and you look at some other women, there is just no question. And if you knew just a little about my personality — I don't really have to fuck every woman that comes along. Especially if they don't turn me on. And given I'm in a situation where all my basic needs are being met, then I don't have a problem. I mean basically, every possible way I could feel was taken care of by one of four different women.

How did Dan deal with the fact that you were sleeping with three other women?

Well, she didn't *know* that. I mean, she knew I had girlfriends. I guess we didn't really talk about it too much. And there was one she didn't even know existed. The only way that it ever came up is she asked me why I was feeling down this particular day. And I said, well, I just told someone I wasn't going to see her anymore. She said, oh, who was that? And I mentioned a name she never heard of.

What was her reaction?

Well, she was kind of surprised. She laughed and got embarrassed — she got kind of dumb. I've only seen her like that about two or three times. And I think I know what it is. Dan thinks — she's smart, right? — she thinks that she understands everything even though I don't tell her. I mean she figures it out.... So I suspect that she was taken aback somewhat. I think she was shocked that she underestimated me.

How long did this situation go on?

I guess until April — March or April. And then I moved in here.

What led to that?

Well... I was living in this studio apartment. I was definitely going to move out of the stuido. I had accumulated so much stuff in a year that clearly I was going to have to move out.... So I began looking for a place, and, well, obviously we had gotten pretty heavily involved. She had this two-bedroom place and she was living by herself. So it was in the back of our minds that this was a possiblity. And it had been intimated before, about living together; in fact, the discussion was, would I get a big enough place? So there was a period of negotiation in April. And... then I just decided that I would move in here. But I was reluctant. I wasn't 100 percent convinced about the whole idea. And she was a little surprised, she didn't think I was going to move in. So....

Did moving in entail no longer seeing these other women?

Well, surely, it would have, and I suppose that's why... I began phasing out those other sexual relationships. You know, even before I began considering a place to live. By the time I moved in, I was not dealing with other women; I was dealing exclusively with Danae.

And how did you work out when you did move in?

It... it was nice. Very smooth.

So whatever doubts you had about it dissipated pretty fast, or....

Yeah. Some of the big, the immediate, serious ones, they dissipated pretty fast. I mean, it must take a long time for people to really "get down" adjusted. I'm still adjusting right now, and it'll be two years in May I guess.

Did it change your relationship in any way, the actual living together every day?

No. We adjusted to one another. But I'm used to her. I would miss her if she were not here. But a lot of things like cooled down. I mean, we just don't stay up till five or six o'clock every night, although we do stay up past two quite often. It's more her than me, so one of the things we're kinda negotiating, we've got to get started earlier. She's the kind of person that requires attention, you know. And you've got to do a lot of talking, and it's none of this bullshit — there are some statistics that the average American married couple has spent something like eighteen or thirty-seven minutes a week interacting. Some ridiculously small amount of time, and it's not that way at all with Danae. It's been a lot of time dealing with things. A lot of talking. A whole hell of a lot of interacting. We just talk about everything. We'll argue and debate... which is good, because I tend to be quiet. I tend to not interact and not deal with a lot of heavy emotions, and I'm learning from Danae.

Is the relationship pretty much the way you want it now, or are the two of you still working at it?

Yeah, we're still negotiating. There's some things she is not happy with. There are some external forces, one being her mother.

Does her mother want her to get married?

Yes, to get married, to be successful. "When are you going to finish school? How come you don't have a job" So I think that Danae's still working through some bullshit that was put on her in her childhood, and in her developing years. So she's working on it. But some of the stuff gets acted out in the relationship, just as I have brought bullshit into this relationship and it gets acted out. So we're working on our respective problems. We just keep talking and at times we have clashes, and we'll argue and fight.

Are there any recurrent themes of discord between you?

Yeah. The word that comes into my mind and the word that I've used is *intolerant*. Danae in my opinion *at times* can be hard and rigid. For instance, once she had a very good friend named David. They were old friends, and she'd always talk about David and she really loves him. And they had an argument about which way you turn the tires in the snow. They just really went at it. Now, admittedly David has problems, but it seems to me if I were her, I wouldn't have insisted on what was the correct answer. But she just took it like it was a *real* important consideration, instead of backing off and letting the guy get away, whether he was right or wrong. I mean, he wasn't going to be convinced that he was wrong. I would say forget it, it's not really worth insisting that your point prevail. I said, "You know, Danae, it seems to me that there's not enough practice. There's too much theory and not enough practice." And by that I mean, if there's a problem to be solved, I tend to go and solve the problem. Whatever it is, let's *do something* to solve the problem, and not a whole bunch of talk about the problem. Just talk, talk, talk and arguing and debating. (The two are supposedly connected.) That and being intolerant. 'Cause I guess it comes off as just a lot of talk, trying to make a point. I think all of that is tied with what happened in coming up and that whole experience in her childhood and growing up and her mom.

Does Danae have any male friends, the way you have female friends?

Uh, yeah, she did, but, you know, she's smart. She just didn't talk about it a whole bunch. It just turned out that I just talked more than she did.

I didn't actually mean boyfriends, but people who were close to her.

Yeah, she had a few, but in thinking about it, she just doesn't have many friends, period. I mean Nina, there's a real good friend of hers. And what that means is that she may talk to Nina once a week, and sometimes twice a week do things together. Nina is about her closest friend, and there are a couple of other women. But... you know, now she doesn't really have a close male friend.

Do you still have very close women friends?

Not really. Not really. We've pretty much absorbed each other.

So you two are self-sufficient?

Yeah, yeah, there's no one that I see regularly. There are a couple of women when I do see them, they're happy to see me, but... it's not like I really *missed* them, that I really needed to see them... and I guess one thing that has happened to me is that I've had a lot of my time occupied with other things. Working and going to school and that kind of thing.

Has the sex changed at all since you've been living together? Has it cooled down after two and a half years?

What do you mean by cooled down? Do I still lust with the same intensity? Well, the element that, of course, is not there is that element of uncertainty which tended to make me more aggressive and more active sexually. Here, she can walk into the room with just a bathrobe on and nothing else underneath and she'll sit down, and I'll see her thigh. I'll get pleasure, but where before I would turn on and deal with that situation immediately, now I know she's going to be here. So I'll look, and I may go and touch her, kiss her on the thigh or something, and go back to cook dinner, and come back and we'll just rap a little bit. So it's different in that way.

How important do you think sex is to the relationship?

Well look, without sex there would not be a relationship. At least not

this kind of relationship. I mean, that's just absolutely clear. But...
other things are also important. That is like saying we have an automobile and we need this automobile to run: now how important are
the tires? How important are the tires vis-à-vis the transmission? Or
the steering wheel? It's like that. It's *important*... you know, but
getting along is even more important. Being friends, I think, is more
important. If we lost the friendship and we could have sex, that
would be a real drag. I think I would just move out, and we'd have a
sexual relationship or something.

Suppose it's the reverse, and you lost the sex but kept the friendship.

Well, I'd have to know how the sex were lost. I mean if I had an acci-
dent and I had my cock and my balls cut off and became a eunuch
or—

**No, I just meant a lot of couples find after a certain period that the
sexual stimulation wears off.**

Uh-huh. Well, you know what I described before could be inter-
preted as the sexual stimulation wearing off. If I see her, I can enjoy
looking at her. In other words, what's happening now is I can get
pleasure out of just looking at her and nothing else. It doesn't have to
be that I look at her and I get excited and we go to bed. I could just
look at her. I can touch her, I can hold her in bed, and not have sex.
Let us say something happened so that we couldn't have sex for two
or three months. Would I leave her? No. Absolutely not. For a year,
no. But I'd make some adjustments. I don't know, I really can't come
up with a good situation.

Do you think about the future much?

Uh-huh. Yeah, I think about it because again there are negotiations
ongoing. At this junction marriage is being considered, and we're
negotiating that. And since Hyde Park is closing up, we're talking
about buying a co-op, which necessitates me becoming more stable.
So we're negotiating things. We're talking about working out some
long-term things. We had a real fight....

How old is Danae?

Twenty-eight. We had a real fight a few weeks back because she announced that she's applying for a job at a psychiatric institute here. If she were to get this job, she'll be living there five nights a week. So I've got to be reasonable and open-minded and all that bullshit, but I really think it sucks. I mean she's there five nights a week and she's going to come home on a weekend and see me? Or on her days off, whenever? Well, that's a real problem, her living there, and I said, "You're going to be there working with men every single day, twelve hours a day interacting and you're talking about you're going to see me on a weekend — how long will that shit last?" So she just says, "Well, look, that's something I got to do." I said, "Well, I hear what you're saying, and I think it sucks." So we have those kinds of situations. And that's still pending. And she's looking for a job in her field. She's never worked; she's never been fully employed in the area that she's been trained in, as a therapist or in social work. So. . . that's got to happen sometime.

Do you see the two-career relationship as creating any particular problems?

Well, we don't have that yet. Not really. She doesn't work and that doesn't bother me, but at the same time I don't want her to turn into a domestic kind of woman. It's a real conflict because I want to have my cake and eat it too. On the one hand I want her to always be available for me and to be here. . . yet I know it's necessary for her to be out in a career. I don't know how I'm going to take that. You talk about being sexually liberated and all that, but when it really comes down to it, I guess I'll adjust. I hope it's not a job like the first one she mentioned, living somewhere else all week and seeing me on Saturday nights, or something where you travel six or seven months out of the year or something like that. I don't know. What I told her is, if she goes into that, the only thing I could do is work my job and maybe go to school full time and just see what happens. That's about all you can do, I guess. I mean I certainly can't say you're not going to take that job. She wouldn't permit that. (Laughter) Our relationship is that I'm in charge and Danae says so. (Long pause) That's about where it's at. (Pause) There's going to be problems, 'cause that's the nature of reality and life and all that, but we've worked out ways of coping with them. I think it has to be that way, because America is just an extremely difficult place to maintain a healthy relationship and to maintain a modicum of sanity and humanity. There's so many pitfalls, there's so many things that are wrong, there's so many pressures placed upon individuals — like the nuclear family — it's a real trip, and... because the traditional institutions are inadequate and people have been cut loose from these institutions, they have to find their own way. And that's a *hell* of a *burden*.

But we're social animals. We're gonna have relationships, we're gonna have families and understandings, and traditions and worries and all this... but it's no longer just given to us or imposed on us; we're not inculcated with how to do this, how we do that — things aren't already worked out. You take something like raising a kid, that's a *titanic* responsibility.... It wasn't that way fifteen years ago, twenty years ago. You didn't have to know so much and today you just don't have the support and the structures that existed twenty years ago.

Do you want to have a family? Do you want to have kids?

Well, I have kids already. Yeah. Now, it's a question we have to negotiate. I *have* three kids. And my youngest is ten. So the question is, am I willing to start all over again? And that's a source of problems. I'm not ready for the diaper stage again. I just can't get excited about it. It's a real problem. Because Danae doesn't have any kids. She wants kids. And she's very clear about that. And the expense of raising one child since the time I first had a child has increased 800 to 900 percent. That's a *real* burden, that's more than a notion. And, of course, I'm in a more difficult situation than someone else, because I support my other kids. A substantial portion of my income goes into maintaining and supporting the three kids I already have. So it's just something that we're dealing with, and I'm not going to procrastinate on the whole issue, so we talk about it. That's where we're at. (Pause) When you ask is sex important to a relationship — no, if this relationship doesn't make it, I think one of the last things it would be is sex. So I guess sex is not really very important. Because with everything that I understand and know, I can give you the order of what would torpedo this relationship, would cause this relationship to fail. And it's not sex. It would be this issue, and some other issue.

The children issue?

Sure, that, right there. (Pause) And as I sit here now, I don't have an answer. And all I know is I turned on the television and I took about six minutes of that and I turned it off. They're talking about double-digit inflation, twenty percent inflation, crime is risen fifty percent and all that — you can't walk the streets. I mean that's where the shit is at. Putting all these people out of work. That is gonna affect this relationship. Because if you have a kid, you gotta have a place to live, and I turn on the news and the banks aren't lending any more money. I would not be able to get a loan to get a house to raise kids in. And I certainly wouldn't bring kids up in a little apartment like this, trying to stay in this area. Raising kids has gotta take so much energy and concern and dedication. It's going to require a very big commitment, and I just don't know if I *can* make that commitment.

Is there any other issue that big in terms of difficulties it might generate?

The biggest issue is that, and the second biggest issue is working out an understanding that would accommodate our long-term objectives, apart from the kids. What we want to do, how we're going to do it, what we're going to be, the job situation and all that, being in careers and being able to maintain our love and our concern and trust.

Would you like to be part of a couple for the rest of your life? Could you also consider living singly?

I could live singly. I have a preference. I prefer living with someone. That's a real preference. I wouldn't want to go through life by myself. Even though there may be some rewards and compensations. Like I could have four or five girlfriends. But I'd rather have a stable, long-term kind of thing. Without all the hassle of the dating scene and calling and you're with one one night, the next night you don't get hooked up and you're by yourself. Some people may say, Hey, that's okay. You know, *occasionally* it's all right. Occasionally I enjoy being by myself, and it would be nice, in this situation, if occasionally I could be alone. And it happens. So far, this month alone, I've spent two weeks not here. That's enough for me. I wasn't looking forward to the couple of days I turned down going to Detroit; I said no thank you: I want to be here. I could have been up in Detroit, living downtown somewhere. I spent nine days in Washington. I spent a week in New York, a couple of weeks before that. And that was enough. But living by myself? No, I wouldn't want to live by myself.

DANAE

Tell me how you met Mark.

Well... it was essentially a modified pickup, modified by his kids. I had never seen him before in my life and within two hours of seeing him for the first time, I was sitting at a meal with him and his children.

How did it happen?

A man had come into the store with these four kids. They were browsing, and I struck up a conversation with the youngest, the only girl child. And somewhere in this their father, this man, was hovering around. She had asked, "Do you go to school at night?" And I said, "No." "Well," she said, "he goes to school at night, just like the Fonz." And that was his cue — or it seemed to be his cue — to introduce himself into the conversation, not to talk to *me*, but to talk to *her*. And say to his daughter, "She seems like a nice lady, how about asking her to join us for pizza after she gets off work?" The kid shook her head up and down, and *then* turned to me. It was the kid's permission first — the invitation was directed toward her. And I said, "Yeah, okay."

Was it clear to you that this was a pickup?

No, it didn't seem like a pickup at all, but that's the reality of it — in the sense that there was no formal introduction. I didn't know this man from Adam. So at five the little girl comes in and tugs on my coat, and we go outside. She immediately let me know who was who by saying how lucky she was to see her father as often as she did, unlike one of her peers. So that let me know that the parents were divorced, and this was their father. And then she also let me know which kid wasn't in the family.

Was his paying for a ninety-cent book by check suspicious to you?

No. First of all, it wasn't a ninety-cent book. What he bought was a *Webster's New World Dictionary* for $7.35 and for somebody to pay by check is *very* normal. Especially people in this neighborhood who are academic professionals, because they take it off their taxes. I didn't think twice about that. *But* what's interesting is that the phone number was his mother's; I later checked it out and looked him up in the phone book. That was his mother's number — not his. But that jumps ahead of the story, I guess. Mark struck me remarkably. I mean he was a very different looking person. I was *immediately* attracted.

From the first moment in the store?

I'd never seen anyone who looked like him before. And I was *immediately* attracted to him. And I didn't even think about the fact that I didn't understand it. I mean, he's not traditionally or characteristically a beautiful man. But I just knew that this was somebody I wanted to know. That's a feeling. . . .

A sexual attraction?

Yes. That was a feeling. . . there are some things about him I appreciate that I have never appreciated in a man before — such as his smell, the feel of his skin, and all of that. Even though those particular aspects weren't apparent in the first moment, that kind of gutsy attraction was there. I don't know what you would call it — juiciness?

So it was the traditional chemical reaction?

I think so. Yeah. At first, he behaved very differently in the restaurant than in the bookstore. He was *very* ill at ease. I asked if something was wrong, and he said, "Yeah, the kids have never seen me with a woman before." He was evasive, too. I asked him if he lived in Hyde Park, and he said no, but near. Well, in Chicago geography, the Loop is *not* near Hyde Park; the North Side is *not* near Hyde Park. Anyway, we left and when we got to the front of my house, he asked which was my window. I showed him, and he said, "Oh you have plants." That meant something to him, that I was a lady who grew plants. And when I got upstairs the first thing I did was call up the bookstore and say, "What's the phone number on that check, and look in the phone book and find out an address." And I thought for all of two hours and then wrote a note inviting him to dinner, saying, "If what you say is true, that you come into this bookstore two or three times a year, the next time I would see you was in July. So how about dinner tomorrow night? Or sometime this week?" And he responded.

Was that an unusual move for you?

(Laughs) I'd written a note once before in my life and it was eight years earlier when I was a freshman in college. So it's not a common thing for me.

Had Mark shown any interest in getting together again, during dinner or on the walk home?

He didn't seem to, but I attributed that to his nervousness about the kids seeing him with a woman for the first time. I knew he was interested, but I can't tell you how I knew it. But I didn't feel that I had a whole lot to lose, or that I was putting myself on the line and would be humiliated or something by sending him the note. That was on a Tuesday, it was March 1, and by the weekend I'd heard from him — in fact, on Sunday morning. And he accepted the invitation. He declined the invitation to come to the house, but he couldn't have known that I had a brother living here and I was chaperoned. I was not inviting a total stranger into my house unchaperoned. My brother would have been there; he may not have sat with us at the meal but he would have been in the house. And the next morning I got another phone call from Mark, who had just come from the bookstore and was told that my days off were Sunday and Monday, which coincided with his days off. And he invited me to join him and his friends who were having breakfast at The Dove. I did and I knew a couple of people who were there, and it was very, very nice. I had somewhere to go right after that, so I was only with them a few hours.

Anyway, prior to this breakfast thing we had made a date on the phone on Sunday for dinner the next Thursday night. And this dinner on Thursday was something I thought a great deal about. I went out and bought a new dress, a Diane von Fürstenberg dress. I also went out and bought a setup of liquor — that's not something I kept in my house. I was prepared to entertain, and he got here and looked shabby. The worst clothes I've ever seen him wear in all the time I've known him. So I changed my clothing to be less elegant and, since he refused to drink anything and there was no excuse to sit in the house, we were out to dinner within ten minutes of his ringing my doorbell.

So we had this meal, which was the first time I realized that he was black. We were talking about traveling, and I asked him, "What kind of name is that? Your last name sounds British. You don't look British, you look Italian or Spanish." And in a bragging kind of way, he let me know how whenever he travels, except to the northern countries like Scandinavia, he fits right into whoever those people are. And he said that he was black and in which way he was black — Cajun and American Indian and all those other things. It didn't matter to me at all, since it's not anything I saw myself. Mark's appearance is such that he could be my brother. That's how I feel and that's a part of the niceness. I don't think I've ever in my life cared for someone who was light-skinned and blonde. I don't remember having a boyfriend that fits that description — the Nordic type. It made no difference to me how it is he got to look like my brother.

How did this dinner go?

What I mostly remember of the dinner was that he was evasive. That was a quality of his I saw, or felt, from the very beginning. He didn't answer directly. I couldn't figure out why. It could have been evasiveness and it could have been, "I have complicated, complex things to say, and you can't just hear one sentence."

It turned out to be evasiveness. He also has complicated complex things to say in his life, but that was evasiveness. What is striking is that he never let me know that he had an involvement anywhere else. At all. The next time I saw him for breakfast, the following Monday, he was much more a full person, he told me much more about his family and his background then. So he eased into self-disclosure very gently.

Anyway, we left dinner, because the restaurant closed at eight, and I thought he'd come here for coffee, but he dropped me at the door asking — this is on a Thursday — how would I like to join that mass get-together with him and his friends for coffee and discussion which they have every Monday. And I was disappointed because it wasn't a date, it wasn't a tête-à-tête. And I came into the house feeling, you know, oh dear, you can forget about that one. Because he did not express his interest — if there was interest — in any of the ways that were familiar to me. He didn't try to extend the evening. He had invited me to dinner, I got my dinner and that was it. He didn't try to ensure a next time. It wasn't really a very definite thing, this Monday breakfast.

But he called me during the weekend to talk while he was on a studio job, and that was a little bit of a surprise. And he asked me my T-shirt size. There was a band there he was taping, and they were giving out T-shirts, and he could get one for me. I thought that was kind of sweet, so he got me a T-shirt. And we made time arrangements for Monday. So it became definite. And there was nobody else there. He took me to a restaurant that's in the little South Side black ghetto. And it was wonderful cheap food. It was a place that I would never feel safe to go to myself, but I was very glad to have been there. It's on Sixty-first and Indiana or something like that, the neighborhood he had grown up in.

He showed me his house. Then we went to a Baskin-Robbins and had an ice cream. And I remember this well. We were sitting on the embankment there, and he asked me how I was feeling. And the answer I gave — I didn't think about it for a second — the word that immediately came out was "contented." And he was surprised. That's not your typical word. But that's really how I was feeling. I mean he was, by then, an attentive, curious man. He was trying to find out a thing or two about me, trying to see who I was. And it wasn't pushy; it wasn't uncomfortable. I did feel contented. But after I had my ice cream, I had to get into my car and drive off to my therapy session. So after that there were phone calls and a steady Monday-with-Mark date.

And all this time he is or is not showing any romantic interest?

Not really. None, actually.

How did you respond to that? It must have seemed peculiar.

Well, since he is older than me by eight years—

You're?

Twenty-eight. Well, then I was twenty-five, about to be twenty-six. I thought maybe it was a function of age. I mean I didn't know how to make sense of it. It felt odd. But what really became difficult was when he started talking about sex, talking about *me* in the context of sex — his feelings for me. That it's something he'd like to do, but he's not *going* to. I really felt toyed with.

What was his explanation for this?

That we should be friends. That is was much more important to develop a friendship than to become lovers prematurely. That's a very nice. . . moral position to take. And maybe it's the way things should be, that people should know each other as friends and make a choice about sex. However, then you don't also tease. And Mark teased.

How?

Well, once I was coming back from a book purchase, and I gave him a call at work. I had a carful of books and I was on my way south and was not too far from where he worked, and it was close to the time a person gets off work. I didn't know his schedule, but it was about four-thirty. So I called him up, and he said he would join me in this restaurant. And he talked about how pretty I was to him. He especially liked my big juicy lips, which is a feature of mine he really likes. He said that he had fantasized about me. And I found the conversation erotic, provocative, seductive, teasing, and very cruel. Because in the same mouthful, he was saying it wasn't going to happen. It couldn't happen. He had this other overriding principle, which was that right now we should be friends, we could talk about anything we wanted, because nothing was on the line. Nothing was on the line for *him*. It wasn't so for *me*. I mean I was agitated, to say the least, by this conversation.

Leaving the restaurant, I was in a high state of tension. As we were crossing the street, he touched the back of my head, and it was shocks. *Shocks* went through my body. And I was really angry at that point. I thought it was very cruel. Not to have touched me inadvertently — although I'm not so sure it was inadvertent — but to have broached the subject in detail and then tell me I couldn't have it. To let me know that he had desires towards me as I did towards him and to let me know it wasn't going to happen. If anything, it was bad manners.

And you were...

I was more confused and hurt than anything else. I think I was angry, and... I was aroused to the point of bitterness. That all he had to do was touch a traditionally non-erotic part, the back of my head, and I was trembling. I mean, I was shuddering.

So, after the incident in the restaurant, you were... confused.

I was confused. I didn't understand. But what was interesting was that after this conversation in the diner, he escalated. I remember one time when we had plans to hear a concert on campus, and we ended up not going because what he did — we were sitting on the floor here and in the middle of some sentence he said, "Can I kiss you?" And I was... because that wasn't supposed to happen. So what Mark had done was increase his repertoire of what was possible without actually having intercourse.

Did you let him?

I said yes, yeah. I guess I did let him.

What was your reaction?

I liked it. I liked it a lot. I mean, he has a very soft mouth and... I've always set great store by a first kiss, unless somebody has been *extremely* nervous. But first kisses.... And my intuitions were sound. I'd already thought he was a sexy man. Sexy in ways that have nothing to do with technique and what he might or might not know, but just in how he walked, how he held himself, his carriage, how he might move his hands or... I don't think you would call this a fetish, but I really like the curve of his neck a lot. It was such a pleasure to watch him. And that was never an important thing for me. I'd always had this... very "noble" view that a person was the person they were inside. But he sure looked *good* to me. I mean, it was like icing — it wasn't icing, it wasn't extra, it was fundamental, actually. It was this new dimension. I was very aroused and very appreciative of him in an aesthetic way.

Before, I thought it was sort of superficial to like somebody because they were handsome. And I didn't like him *only* because he was handsome to me, and as I said, he's probably not traditionally good-looking. But that was an inalienable part — how he moved, how he talked, the sound of his voice, the curve of his neck — that was an inalienable part of him. And it's the first time I'd ever had them together.

How is he different from your previous romantic and/or sexual experience?

Well, I'd had many boyfriends. I mean I didn't "date," I don't know if people do that anymore, but... it's a funny thing, because when you're attractive, you're in a position of choice. I know that *now*, but I didn't act upon it then. I don't think I knew it then. I was always surprised that I didn't have to be alone.

Had you been in love before?

Yes. (Pause) My first lover I knew for two years; that started when I was sixteen and ended when I came to college. Why I came to college was not to have to marry this man. And a few months after being in school I met somebody I liked, and we stayed together, living together in the dorm. He was also a couple of years older than me. That relationship lasted from Thanksgiving of one year to September almost two years later. It was a curious thing because he was not physically attracted to me. I know, because he said it. Because I asked. I mean I *knew* something was off. He liked long-legged, high-assed, slender blonde women. I was not that and I wondered why he was with me. But we played together a lot. He was a musician in a band, and I became very close friends with the girlfriend of somebody else in the band. We were a foursome and we had a *lot* of fun. More fun than I'd ever had in my life before that. And it was... I was young, it was a lot of fun.

Sex wasn't such a big part of that relationship. He wasn't that attracted to me. I'd never had an orgasm. And I wasn't about to with him, either. I... when I look back, I realize how close I had always been and I think that what would have made the big difference was knowing that he valued my appearance. We all have problems. So... he leaves Chicago, and I'd had an affair towards the tail end of that relationship, when he stopped sleeping with me completely. That was with a man who was younger than I was, and it was probably the first, last, and only mystical experience I'm ever going to have. I mean this relationship was filled with roses and Gabriel Rossetti and the whole works. I loved it. And when there was a breach in that relationship which I didn't understand, I didn't know what it was about, but I was going to kill myself over it, because this was "The Sorrows of Werther" kind of thing. (Laughing) And it was a serious debate for me whether I was of the element of air or of the element of water. And thank goodness I opted for water, because I threw myself into Lake Michigan, and it was frightening because it was cold and scary. I don't know how I got out. I... when I got out, my knees were scraped, my legs were scraped, I was in a silk dress. I was cut up on my arms and legs. I mean, I felt I had thrown myself into the water, but the water didn't want me. But... well... it was kind of magical, because the enormity of what I had almost done did not impinge upon me at all. (Laughing) Not in the least. I... he was too ethereal for me.

So we come back to Mark and his sexual tease.

I liked it. What can I say? There were many, many long goodbyes at the door. And I... my notion of passion is that it's an overcoming of barriers. It's the intensity, the heat in trying to make the barriers between the two of you not be there. There's an obstacle of some sort that has to be overcome. Well, the obstacle at that time was very, very clear. Mark said no, and I wanted yes.

How long did this period go on?

Probably six weeks. Actually, the first time we had sex was inadvertent. We had already developed to the point... he had escalated what was permissible. I mean, he kept changing the ground rules on what was permissible without...

Having sex.

Without having sex. But we had gotten to bed by then. And that really was like high school — making out in the backseat. Except the roles were changed. (Laughing) Here I was wanting to do something, and he was the shy I'm-not-going-to-give-it-up-yet type.

How did you actually get to bed?

The first time was curious. We were by the door. And I... see, in this building you can hear somebody coming into the major hallway, and it's hard to know whether they're about to come into the apartment or not, and my brother was expected any minute. So we're standing by the door, and I'm really very keyed up, and I heard the outside door opening. I said, "Oh, that's my brother," and took Mark by the hand and pulled him into the bedroom. And he just went along, and here we are in bed. And we were just lying on the bed kind of still, and he said, "You know, it feels like I've been with you ten years." We were both fully dressed. And it was nice, feeling his hair on my cheek, and it was wonderful holding him. Something surprising happened then, which is that I had an orgasm and didn't know it was happening, and he didn't know it was about to happen, he wasn't even doing anything directly to make it happen.

Just from lying together?

No, he was kissing me, he was kissing me... he was kissing my leg, but he wasn't in contact with my genitals at all. And it was explosive. (Pause) It was a surprise. There was no plateau, no buildup or anything like that, it just suddenly seemed to *happen*. But then again, you know, you stand in front of the doorway for forty-five minutes saying good-bye and embracing...

Were you aware how much this was a reversal of the traditional role situation?

No. Uh-uh. I mean... that has more to do with notions of self-worth than anything else. It's taken me many, many years to be comfortable with being a pretty woman. To take some credit for that, and not just simply say it has to do with my genes. When I first came to the university at eighteen, *I was shocked* — and this after having a lover for two years who was ten years older than me — but I was *shocked* at some of the response I got, especially from blacks. It was such a surprise to me. What I'm trying to say is. . . this did not strike me as being a role reversal because I had less feelings of entitlement than I might have had. To think of it as a role reversal means that you have to understand what the roles are, you have to feel entitled to your role — mainly that you should be pursued. You're the woman and you should be pursued. But. . . since it's taken me *so* many years to. . . and I don't still feel that way, either. . . it was not in my consciousness that this was a role reversal. Probably because none of my liaisons seemed to have conformed to what the roles were supposed to be. I mean. . . when men approached me, either they were smart and they could talk and they were dynamic, or I wasn't interested. As for the sexual component and who pursued — I did as much pursuing in my life as being pursued. If Mark experienced it as a role reversal, it's because he was going to do something different than what he thought this pretty woman was accustomed to. But this pretty woman wasn't accustomed to too much.

What happened after that?

I don't really remember. (Pause) I remember the second time we got into bed and I thought it was going to be the same thing, and at one point he just said, "Oh, what the hell," or something like that. And disrobed and it was over very quickly. He must have been extremely anxious. I was surprised. (Pause)

How was that as sex?

It was more nervousness than anything else. I think he was very nervous. I didn't make a big deal about "hey, what about me?" Because it was pretty clear that this was a big deal. I mean, I thought that, given all the buildup, he would have been more formal or more — it wouldn't have been yielding to an impulse the very first time we had intercourse. It would have been something more staged than it was. But it was a "Oh, what the hell" kind of thing. I was a little surprised. That it was kind of inadvertent. Then we went home. I mean, he went home.

And the fact that he went home. . . .

I didn't like it.

Did you think about it?

Sure I did. But by then I already knew that he was living with somebody.

When did you find that out?

Probably three, four weeks into knowing him. It was a couple of weeks before our first lovemaking. I . . . asked questions. I mean, what I asked for was his phone number, and what I got from him was this big fanfare about how I was going to be given his very special private number at the studio, as opposed to the NBC switchboard. I'm sure he doesn't remember this. And I said, "That's fine." I was gracious about it. Then I said, "How about your home number?" He said I had his home number. I said, "No, that's your mother's number, you don't live there. Do you live with your mother?" And he said no. And he said, "I can't give you that number. I live with someone." No, he said, "I can't give you that number. I have a good reason." I said, "Yeah, that reason is that you're living with somebody, aren't you?" He hesitated, then he said, "Yes." And I was shattered. I was really shattered.

Did you suspect this was the case before he told you?

I was selectively naive. I . . . I mean, I really didn't have a suspicion. What can I tell you? I mean things didn't jive, I thought he had something to cover. It never occurred to me it was *that*. Some other more crafty woman would have figured it out right away. I'm sure that if I were hearing some other woman tell me about this man and his behavior, I would have jumped to that conclusion immediately. But I didn't. I didn't. So I was *really* stunned. I felt an enormous amount of disappointment because things were not as they had seemed. There was a clear, mundane, banal reason he was keeping his distance. Somebody else was in the picture. It had nothing to do with developing a friendship; it had to do with not wanting to blow your cover. Or ruin anything for yourself. So I felt deceived. I felt betrayed.

How did you react when he told you?

I was very polite. I terminated the conversation. I basically said I felt that he had lied to me, that he had betrayed me. And I didn't want to hear, as he started to tell me, that this was just a roommate, he'd needed a place to live, she had a room, they worked together, so on and so forth. Because if it's a roommate, then you can give your phone number. And what I said was, "No, you were protecting her interest. You must be romantically involved. I don't want to hear that you're not. Don't tell me it's a roommate."

So he initially tried to lie?

Yeah, he did. Well. . . it's a technical lie, not a psychological lie. For more than a year he had been trying to say goodbye, and this woman had a full armament of ways to keep somebody there — guilt, "My mother's dying," "You can't do this to me," "This is not what you said was going to happen," and so on and so forth. He *wanted* to leave, so in *his* eyes he was just a boarder there. But. . . what I see is that it's not too different than somebody on their way to being divorced saying they never were married, when what's really going on is that they're getting a divorce. Why not say you're getting divorced, or that you are in fact married but it's going to end? What he was saying was analogous to saying I'm not married. Just because he felt not married, but technically he was still married.

It was the dissembling that bothered me. I mean, it wasn't a situation that I could not live with, and as it turned out I did live with it. For quite some time. It was his distortion that really bothered me. And rather than make myself crazy wondering about it, because sometimes his first answer would not be the true answer, and rather than nagging and asking the question many times, I just developed a technique. "Whatever you say now, I'm going to believe." And he would then be free to say whatever he wanted to say. But he was going to be held responsible for it. If that's the version he was going to give me, then dammit, he was going to be held responsible for it. I don't want any qualifications later. Because I'm going to believe it and I'm going to act on these premises. I don't think I ever found out otherwise once I'd hit upon that technique.

But how was it left at the time, this Sunday morning when you found out he was living with someone?

I was in a stupor I think. I said I would like to get off the phone now. And he said all right. I was angry, and he heard some of the anger. But nothing was said about breaking the standing Monday morning date. I don't remember whether it was that Sunday or the following day, but we hashed it out for a long time. Until I really got the story straight of where he was, why he was there. And you know, some of my anger dissipated, because basically he said, "Look, I didn't know who you were; if I really told you the truth, you may have said to me, 'I never want to know you. Don't come around till you get rid of her.'" So it was... flattering in a way. He was saying. "Because I wanted to know you, I just felt this was a safer risk than telling you the truth." Now, as it turns out, a person will always win with me if it's the truth. He didn't know that. That's a lesson he's had to learn again and again with me. What I cannot tolerate is lying. Any kind of lying. Unless it's something that you don't know yourself, that is not available to you. I mean, I don't smack him on the head because he's got an unconscious. But where he's aware of the duplicity, I get angry.

So he told you he was trying to get out of this relationship?

Right. And I didn't like being in that position for myself. It's a funny thing, because I wanted to be with him, and yet I also enjoyed the idea of somebody having a clear moral position. He'd explained the situation sufficiently so that I understood that I was not threatened by this relationship that existed before he knew me. That relationship was hearing its death knells. But I just didn't like the fuzziness. . . .

Did you ask him how long it would take to be over?

Well, he made it sound like it was any minute; they had already started talking about his *really* moving out. He also told me that he wasn't sleeping with her anymore. And I know that that's possible, that you could be in the same bed with somebody and not be sleeping with them. So I believed him.

This was the end of April. Well, June 1 he moved out. It wasn't a whole lot of time. And I knew he was looking for an apartment... but one night he was here, maybe two weeks later, and I said goodbye to him. I don't remember what motivated me to do it, but I did say goodbye to him and I remember him standing up and saying, "This is a terrible way for us to end. This is a *horrible* way." I mean, we had just made some wonderful kind of love, and I'd said goodbye to him. I don't remember too much about that. I do remember that the next day I got a phone call from the bookstore saying that there was a plant there, from Mark.

Then Mark called and asked my advice about whether he should move into some building and what did I think about that location? He had this way of completely skirting and avoiding whatever the issue was, or whatever the crisis was, and just neutralizing it. So I got sucked into giving him advice about what apartment he was going to take. But what he was doing was letting me know he was in the rental market. So, in due course, he does move out... and that part of the relationship I'll be damned if I understand at all. Here he was out of her house, but he wasn't pursuing me. There were weeks on end, maybe ten days on end, where I wouldn't see him.

His reasoning was now that he knew he was leaving her, he was going to have his own place. Since the day he was born, he's always lived with a woman, whether it was his mother or his wife. He'd never lived alone. And he thought he should really do that, it was something he needed to do for himself. And I understood that. I felt it like a punch in the stomach, but I really understood it. I thought it was foolish. I said to him, he was throwing happiness away with both hands. But, you know, people make foolish mistakes 'cause... I mean, I understood it. I guess that was his way of protecting himself, insuring that he do this thing in the world that he thought he needed to do, which is take care of himself. Learn how to wash a glass. Sew some socks.

What was your reaction to that? After three months of your relationship he's actually moving out on this other woman....

And he's not seeing me.

And saying at that point, I need time to be alone more, so I'm not going to see you. How did you react?

What was my reaction? There was nothing I could do about it. I thought he was a jerk. I told him I thought he was a jerk. What could I do about it? He said that's what he was going to do. He didn't tell me about it in my home, where I might have felt much more comfortable about screaming at him and maybe even socking him. He told me in a restaurant.

Did you think it was really over?

Yeah. I did. See, I believed him. (Laughs) That's probably why I still know him, I took him at his word. The man says he has some growing to do and I believed that. And I was fortunate to have my brother here who said, "You can't push that. The man is saying that this is what he needs, and whether he's wrong to need it or not, that's what he thinks he needs. Don't call him up, leave him alone." But Mark reintroduced himself into my life in a very cavalier way, at which point I did get angry.

How?

He came to the bookstore. Whenever he had some serious business to communicate in those early days, he did it when there were other people around and my response would be inhibited. So he came into the bookstore.

I was surprised to see him. I was *stunned*, and I walked out of the store. Then he called me at home and said, "Can I talk to you?" And he pushed me to give him an answer. I said yes . . . or I said no, I don't remember. I do remember that he called me up at home, and I said, "Fuck you." I was furious, I was screaming at him over the phone. And he said he really needed to talk about what had happened. I said, "Okay, but not here." He said he had to see his kids, that he'd be free at eight o'clock. Well, I decided I was not going to wait for him without doing anything. I had to discharge something. I really didn't want to see him in the house. I was afraid that he would sweet-talk — one way of looking at it is "sweet-talk," another way of looking at it is that's he's Oil Can Harry — and that he would somehow insinuate himself back into bed and that I would not be able to resist. I didn't want that to happen until I had a chance to vent some spleen.

We agreed to meet at Jimmy's, the university bar. I don't remember that conversation too much. He really didn't have a legitimate reason for seeing me now or explaining why he had changed his mind or anything like that. It was just somehow... I'd like to say that we were back on track, but that wasn't quite it. Something had soured for me. But I didn't make a stink about it. I mean, I didn't nail him. But then what followed was that he wasn't seeing me very often. The whole summer went by that way. That I just wasn't seeing him often.

Once a week, once every two weeks?

Sometimes it might be twice a week and sometimes it might not be for ten days. I don't know what the hell he was doing. (Pause) See, this was still prior to his moving into his own apartment, and he was very filled with himself. He was into buying towels and buying dishes and picking out furniture and things like that. It was kind of touching. So that was the first excuse for why I wasn't getting the attention I felt I should be getting.

But by the end of June, he'd been in his house a month, he was settled in. I started getting really unhappy, 'cause I wasn't seeing him very often. And I was taking a course in the Loop at Roosevelt University and I remember many times calling him up from downtown, saying Can I come by? I guess he didn't have to make a point of seeing me, because I always managed to do it. As I'd get out of class, I'd have the impulse to call him up and I would. And he said yes. I don't think he ever said no. Those times. Now his claim was that he was waiting for me to do it. He knew he would see me on those nights, that I would give him a call. So I guess it's.... And *then* he announced that he was taking a trip with this woman.

The trip to the Iberian peninsula?

Yeah. Nothing had changed in how often I saw him. It was still occasional, erratic... maybe five or seven times a month. But we're only talking about two or three months. Well, when he told me that, I set things up in such a way that I was going to leave first. I went to California.

How did you feel about his traveling with this woman?

Well, he had given his reason for it, which was the tickets were paid for. They were going on a charter, a group thing, and the tickets were paid for. See, if you give me an excuse that has to do with large sums of money, I'm going to buy it. Being working-class, I know that money isn't something that comes to people too easily. I'm not going to have this false standard there. I didn't like it, but there was no way I could argue against it. He just doesn't have that kind of money to throw away. What could I say?

So you arranged to leave the city first?

That's right, so he could experience *my* leaving. I was hurt. I wanted to go away. And it had the added advantage that he would have to experience my leaving him first. But my prime motivation was, "*Shit*, this is *terrible*. I don't want to be here anymore. I want to do something diversionary." I had been planning this trip anyway, but I had planned it for September, which was coincidentally the same time Mark would have been away. But my scheduled departure date was after Mark would have left. And I didn't want to wait. So I left and I missed the hell out of him. There was something about watching the Pacific and being on a nude beach for the first time. I just wished he was there to be with me, to enjoy these things with me. I had the continuous feeling of turning to him and saying, "Ain't that something?"

So, I came back early. He was still here. He picked me up at the airport. I was supposed to stay two weeks; I think I stayed six days. Six, seven days. . . .

So you came back, and. . . ?

He picked me up at the airport and he did a dumb thing again, or nasty thing. I mean, I don't always want to attribute malicious motivations to him, but you *wonder* sometimes. He knew what flight I was coming in on, and *he wasn't there*. He just *wasn't there*. I stood there. I looked around, I waited, I stood in front of the men's bathroom thinking he might come out, I looked at the phones. I mean, he wasn't there. And I finally went to get my luggage, and there he was holding my luggage. Yeah. Well, that's an extra fifteen, twenty minutes of turmoil that just wasn't necessary, it was *thought-less* on his part.

I had promised, If he picks me up, I'd buy him breakfast, but my plane was late so we didn't have time for breakfast. We came to the house, we made love, and he went to work. And he left within the week. I got a couple of postcards from him. Not until late in his trip.

Less than a week after his return, I said I just wasn't going to see him anymore. I had started school, which was probably why I had the courage to do this. I had something I was interested in, unlike the deadness of the bookstore by then. I said, "I'm not going to see you anymore," because enough was enough. I mean, you haven't seen somebody for six weeks, you would think that when they came back, there would be some intensity — there would be many, many times that you would see that person initially and then you might taper off. But it wasn't the case. He went back into his silly-ass thing. He saw me immediately, and then he didn't see me for a few days. And then it was another week after that that I didn't see him. I said, "I can't do this. We're exactly where we were, and it seems to have made no difference that you weren't with me for six weeks. And as I said to you before: I don't think it's second fiddle; I feel like I'm not in the orchestra."

Well, he didn't believe me. He came by the bookstore a couple of times, he called the house a couple of times. He stopped trying after a week or so, two weeks at the most. I mean, it wasn't like he was trying a whole lot, he didn't put himself out on a limb by having the door slammed in his face too often. And I really don't think I would have yielded had he been more persistent, because I saw no future in it. I saw no reason that this would ever change. Whatever it was was apparently comfortable for him, but it was not comfortable for me. And I wasn't going to win. There was no ploy I could use. There was no way to draw him to me, no way to threaten him. It had to be over. And it was. For three months.

From October to December you didn't see him?

Uh-huh. (Pause) Uh-huh. (Pause)

How did you feel in those three months?

I was sad about it, but you know, it's a funny thing. After the first week goes by and then the second week goes by, it's duller. It's duller. But it was not being done to me, it was something I did for myself. I had put an end to my being a leaf tossed around by the wind. I put my life back into... some sort of shape. I may not like the situation I'm in — I don't know Mark anymore — but the other situation was intolerable, and not knowing him now was of my own doing. So if I didn't like it, that's tough noogies for me. I thought I would never see him again.

Did you see anybody else in that period?

It's the damndest thing. Here you are in school — you're a graduate student, and fifty percent of your class is men — and you think there's some chance of finding somebody in this situation — after all, it's not a random selection of people. You're in the same program. You have the same interest. You want to do the same thing in the world. There wasn't a man to be found. A grown-up adult man to be found. Now that could be because I was two or three years older than most people, because I had been working between my B.A. and going to graduate school. But there wasn't an adult there. Not one. I dated somebody who was not from the school, and it was nothing. It just was nothing. I mean I was going through the motions. And it wasn't even pleasant. Now that I think about it, I was pretty celibate. There wasn't anybody really. Luckily I had friends throughout this. I had support. It could have been worse. And in that period, I had school to occupy me. And I did school furiously then.

How did this period come to an end?

Well (sighs), really what happened was that one night I got plastered. Which was rare. And I called him up late at night, after the bar closed. It was probably two in the morning. I called him up, and he said that he had tried to reach me many times, but I never answered the phone. And I said Okay, officially let's assume that this time you've reached me. And he said let's get together.

Oh wait... it was a stupid thing again, he put it off a few days. It was Friday night, and he said I can't see you Saturday night — I'll see you Sunday. I thought, oh shit, what's he doing Saturday night that he can't see me? And as it turned out, he couldn't see me Saturday night because even though he was living alone, he had a standing date Saturday night with the woman he used to live with. I don't know how she put up with it, but she did. He saw her once a week, Saturday night, and he was gone by one o'clock in the afternoon. But she was holding on to straws.

So you saw him Sunday — how was that?

I was annoyed because, all right, first he looked good. I wondered whether I hadn't made a mistake because he had no plans for dinner or anything like that. I mean, he was going to come over and shoot the breeze or get in bed. And I wasn't sure that I wanted to do that immediately. I mean, three months is a long time. So I insisted we go out to dinner... immediately we started seeing each other every single night. And I remember the event that made it official. One night we went out, and he said he had some work to do, and I said fine, and he drove me home. So here I'm at my house, and it's eleven o'clock. Fifteen minutes later I get a phone call from him, and he says, "I didn't have *that* much work to do, why don't you come over?"

So after that, generally, he would pick me up at seven, after he had shopped for dinner, which he would cook. And that's an important feature because it explains some of our tension — our discord when he moved in. Mark did everything. I was always a guest in his house. I'd walk in, and he would go to the kitchen, and I would just fold up the bed and straighten up the living room, empty out the ashtrays. And that was it. He purchased the dinner. He made dinner. He washed the dishes. I mean occasionally I did things like that, but I wasn't expected to. I was a guest in his house. And he kept a very neat house. I never used the vacuum cleaner or washed his windows. He did that. Which made it an *enormous* surprise when he moved in here and we started living together, and he pulled this macho chauvinistic kind of thing — you're the woman, you do it. I was a student then, and I had a job, *too*. I was working thirty hours a week. And there was no division of labor which had been contracted for.

But for this year when you were visiting him almost nightly in his house?

Well, I would study until dinner was ready; sometimes he would go visit his friends. There were several women who lived on his floor who he was good buddies with. They did not like it at all that I was a white woman. They were just pissed at that. Well, they'd had him all summer to themselves. This was a new thing for Mark too. He had never had women friends to play with. They were pretty upset because it was clear that one, we were having sex, and two, I was white.

So you were there every night for a year?

Pretty close. The number of times I slept alone I could count on my two hands. For the first month and a half, he was still doing his Saturday night thing with the woman he used to live with. Until one night I was very depressed, it was Saturday, he had picked up his kids, called me from his mother's house, asked me what I was going to be doing that night, and I started crying. Because I didn't like it that he was going there. And he called back and said, Okay, tonight he was going to tell her that it was never going to happen again. I was relieved when it was over, and I was really shocked to find out that he was saying goodbye to *three* people — not one but *three!*

How did the issue come up of his moving in here with you?

Well, there were four months of my never being in my own house. We both wanted to be with each other during non-working hours, so it seemed foolish to me to continue this. I think I was the pusher in that. I mean I know I was a pusher in that. It made no sense. We *were* together. And we should be together. And it was inconvenient. I was using my house as a closet, and I wanted to be in my house. Mark had a very comfortable house and all, but still, my schoolwork was suffering, and I had another year to go. So I thought the best solution would be... that we would have an *our* house. That there should be an "our." So we looked around. We thought the best thing was to find a new apartment, and both of us move from our old houses into that. Mark has some very strong feelings about not being a squatter in a woman's house.

So we did try to look for a third apartment. But it turned out that this was the best we were going to do, and what's more, this was pretty good. I mean this is a very good deal. Once you look at the market, this apartment just looks so much better. And I gave up a study, so he had a room for his kids to come to. That was an issue. I know I've not gone into his turmoil about whether or not he should live with me. He had arguments against it, but I don't remember his arguments against it too well. (Laughs) I knew what I wanted, and ah... it happened. I don't know exactly how it got to that.

What happened when he moved in?

Well the first indication of problems was that he in no way coordinated his moving date with my life. He moved in during the middle of my exams. He just didn't ask me about it. He said, "This is when it's good for me; I can take this week off." And I resented that, but I thought, "Shit, I'm getting so much, let it slide." Well, when he moved in, he spent an enormous amount of time fixing up the study. That was his room. And he didn't really spend too much time in the rest of the house.

After a couple of months, I realized the man never goes into the kitchen unless he's invited. Unless there's a meal on the table. I mean Mark was wonderful at his house about these after-sex feasts. He had all sorts of delicious things, little shrimps, stuff I could never afford on my own. He'd make these *fantastic* combinations of things. And here he didn't even go into the kitchen.

I finally started saying that I noticed that was going on. Does he really feel that he doesn't live here? We discussed that. It took him a long time to make this his house. And we did some mechanical things like shop together. Or I would do the shopping and let him know what was in the cabinets, so he would feel comfortable about going in there. And at first I cooked a lot. And that's... this is a great sadness in our relationship. I'm a really good cook, an excellent cook. But Mark doesn't like my food. I mean, what he says is that he's unaccustomed to Greek food, to those tastes. He's unaccustomed to tomatoes. And I don't know. So I have become somewhat adept at things I've never made before in my life. Like pork chops or roast beef or fried chicken. There's a lot of pain involved in that, because I love to cook Greek food and I'm very good at it.

How did you deal with this?

Oh, well, we fought about it. There were several times when I just told him what I thought was what, that he was a chauvinist, that he went through a whole long thing that women were slaves because that's what his mother was, that once he felt secure in a relationship he could be selfish... and things like that. We fought about it a lot. Well, Mark was never liberated, never.

So we made an agreement. Instead of my paying half the rent and expecting that he do half the things in the house, since I had left my job for school, I stopped paying half the rent and I started doing everything in the house. And where we've had difficulties, they're not enormous — it's just a question of thoughtfulness. You just spent two hours cleaning up the kitchen, and it's spotless and somebody goes in there and makes something to eat, they can put the bread away. Or they can take a rag and wipe the crumbs and the mayonnaise off the counter.

Another problem was he finished work at five or six, and I wasn't finished, I had studying to do. So he felt gypped. He felt that he didn't have access to me. I think it's bad when that happens, when your schedules aren't similar, or the amount of work that you've committed to do in the world isn't similar. So he got himself registered for school. And then it was okay. Then it was, "Don't bother me; I'm reading." (Laughs)

And we haven't talked about his kids at all. That's a big feature in this relationship. But I just started training the kids, appealing to their sense of fairness. That they should pick up after themselves: "Carry your glass into the kitchen and run some water in it. I'm not asking you to wash and dry it or put it away, but don't leave the milk so when I go in there I've got cruddy dishes." They were *much* more responsive than he was. And when he started going to school, he *still* didn't do things, but he wasn't making those extra demands on me. Because he was busy.

Also he flourished. It's an amazing thing about him that he has continued to grow. Many of his attitudes have altered. He's come to see that he was just silly, that somebody imposed this set of beliefs on him and they don't work. He's grown a lot. Just when I think I know him, he comes to some insight or he does something and I think he's more wonderful than I thought. He's continuously growing in this relationship. And it hasn't been easy.

You know, Mark behaved in such ways that, if you use the usual barometers, I shouldn't be here. I mean he put me through the wringer. That's true, but I always thought it was out of conflict. His behavior — not calling me and the deception and things like that — just simply did not seem congruent with who he was in interaction with me. Mainly what I saw in him was his better self. I suppose what I'm saying is he was highly moral. So I never really believed that shit he was putting me through was him.

See, the remarkable thing about Mark is that he never denies reality. It's painful for him to see that he has notions which, well, they're silly or they're bullshit or they're based on prejudices and socialization. Mark doesn't make himself blind to things around him or his own behavior because it's uncomfortable. He is willing to confront aspects of himself that he finds deplorable. Now that's admirable. He has a quality of introspection and a scrupulous kind of self honesty that I find admirable. In that context, people can grow; he can grow. And I've seen it.

What I'm talking about is attitudes, the premises upon which he bases his action, and in some regards he's a sexist. Now he has come to see that. It's not been pleasant for him, it's not been comfortable, but he has come to see that that's the case. And if a person is actually a whole piece, then you can make alterations without actually cutting yourself up. And he's been able to do that.

What I'm trying to say is that because some of his beliefs are so strong, he will not tolerate bad behavior in himself. So all I did was hold him to his better self. It was a gamble, and it worked. It was worth it; it was well worth it. And while his not showing up and things like that were difficult to get through, I always had the feeling that he had actual respect for me as a person. That he had an appreciation for the differences that are me. And he took enjoyment from who I was.

What's happened now is certain problems have surfaced. Partly because I've been interested in taking a job that will keep me out of the house for four nights a week. That's forced him to reassess a lot of things and to realize that he needs me. And that's an injury for somebody who hasn't thought that about himself. You know, just a little while ago he said he was going to leave me.

Over?

Well, he said he didn't *like* me. He wasn't happy. It was over nothing substantial. Nothing I could put my hands on and say that's a reason. Truthfully, over the fact that I wasn't going to be around a lot. That's my interpretation. Well, fortunately I didn't scream. I didn't know what to do. I saw so clearly that he was suffering, and I didn't know what to do. I went to touch him and I stopped and said, "Mark, you have to help me here, because I don't know if you want to be left alone, I don't want to do anything that's a violation to you." This had gone on for two hours until I said that, and he said, "That's the first thing that you've said that's made sense all evening. That's the first thing you've said that's made sense all week. *All month.*" So what he told me was, I *do* want to be left alone. I went and took a bath. I came back into the room and sat quietly and then he started telling me what was troubling him. I just figure that's his stuff, and when he wants to start talking about it, he will. (Pause)

And, you know, sometimes it's a Tuesday night — it ain't a Saturday night, it ain't a Friday night, it ain't a date night. And we're sitting here with music in the back, and we're talking, and I'll just stop. And I'll realize, damn, this is a Tuesday night, I'm in *my* house and I'm having a *wonderful* time.

I don't know if I can really convey that. I'll give you an example. It's a trivial one, but maybe it captures it. I remember one conversation. Sometimes things pop in your head and you say them? I said, "How is it that the record needle picks up the sound we hear?" 'Cause that's something he might know about. Well, after getting the technical stuff down, within a few hours, we were talking about what... what at one time was called natural philosophy. It was a philosophical discussion. And it had started out from something about atoms and sound and needles and tape decks, I mean, grooves and impressions, etc. And we got into a discussion that had to do with how is the world made. That happens a lot. Part of what I was talking about is that we talk to each other, not just about how we feel and the relationship, but about the world.

So... things that have nothing to do with him, he's been able to talk about with me. And I've been able to grow with him. Like I'm bellyaching about the fact that I have to leave therapy, I'm terminating. I mean this is the right decision, the time is up. And he makes the analogy to physical therapy. He makes it so clear to me — in an emotional way, not just a cognitive way — that I was absolutely doing injustice to myself if I protracted this any longer. Making that analogy in the way that he did, in the language that spoke to me, made me realize I was doing absolutely the right thing. The whole point of therapy was to be free of it. I should get out. I was ready to terminate.

Mark and I *talk* to each other. The kids are kind of amazed about it, too, they notice it a lot. (Pause) I'm never going to be bored with him, and that's very different than somebody who always needs stimulation. It's very different. I'm not talking about kicks or thrills or anything like that. I'm talking about a day in, day out thing. I talked before about what I felt passion was, like a successful over-coming of boundaries. Now the more you live with someone, the more you don't have boundaries, there's a certain kind of sharing the same wavelength, to use a cliché. So that immediate kind of passion that's predicated upon strife, upon having to overcome the boundaries, that struggle gets diminished. But it's a trade-in that we seem willing to make. Namely, that there's a lot of joy in being in concert with each other. I am continuously interested in what his opinion might be. Things happen to me during the day, and it's with a sense of anticipation that I come home and want to tell him about it.

I said that I think we've made a trade-in for intimacy. Now this peculiarly rich sexual attraction — and it's rich and new for me — I'm smart enough to know that when I'm fifty-five years old, I ain't gonna look the way I do and I'm probably not gonna feel the way I do. And I am willing that that should diminish. It has to. Because the passion goes away. Because the boundaries are no longer in existence. You know, husband and wife go down the street, they see the same event and they're on the same wavelength, they merge. Well, I'm going to get old. And that sexual stuff is going to wear itself thin in some ways that I can't predict. I believe that. And it really comes down to the issue of commitment.

What we have experienced since living together is that there's an ebb and a flow. There are times that we live a parallel existence, having a nodding acknowledgment of the other person's presence. Then there are times we look up and realize that the other person is there, and it's as hot as the beginning. I think what happens to us is that we fall in and out of love with each other. I think it has to do with both our crazies and both our problems outside the relationship. Two or three times I have thought, "I don't care for this man, I don't like this man. This man is limiting me," etc. And then he'll do something or say something or show me something and I say, "That's *wonderful!*" And it's back again. It's a new love all over. By now I am convinced that it's worth riding out the difficult times, because there will be that pitch again. He's not touching me for a week, but he will. And it will be as it should be, it'll be *nice*, it'll be *good* for me.

All I'm trying to say is that I have managed to learn — and I don't know whether he has, but I have managed to learn — that it's *okay* for him not to want me. That it doesn't mean he doesn't *want* me categorically. That it's *okay* for him not to be up to his usual self. And that's a new thing for me. I would have broken up with somebody the first or second time they didn't seem to be treating me well or liking me very much. I couldn't have tolerated it. Now with Mark, I believe that he is a constant man. So he's got moods just like the rest of us. I give Mark credit for this too: when I wasn't feeling loved and appreciated, for some reason, just by *telling* him I wasn't feeling loved and appreciated, we got out of it. Somehow from the very beginning there was a *possibility of discussion.* So I learned not to act out with him. In the beginning there were times I wanted to run away. Well, to my great surprise, I found I could tell him how I was feeling. Tell him that what he did just hurt the shit out of me and does he know it? And my telling him allowed him to regulate himself, and vice versa. I didn't scream, I didn't shout, I didn't say all the things that once you say you can never erase saying. That happened a couple of times, and I really hurt him. I didn't mean to and I was so ashamed, and I didn't do it again. I kept control out of respect for him. The magic of all this for both of us is that we have ceased to believe one person can read the other person's mind. Now it's wonderful, especially in bed, when he happens to hit upon exactly the thing that I was about to ask for. But that's fairy tale stuff. It really is. And we know that. So we are both teaching the other person continuously, "I can't read your mind. I am *not* you. Tell me, and if I can help, I will do my damndest to."

What about the times when Mark means to hurt you....

Then he gets a fight. When there are times, and there are times, that he is actually willfully malicious. Well, I say, "You know, Daddy, you're a grown-up, and goddamit, I'm going to hit you back, and let's hope that you can tell me what's wrong." But I don't put up with it. I'm not a victim. When he's being nasty, I call him on it.

I wondered about the fact that being an interracial couple does not seem to have caused many problems.

I told you why it didn't.

You didn't know that he was black for a while.

Yeah, but it's not just that. It's that... I think part of my attraction to a person is that they mirror me physically. I love it that Mark's skin color and his hair color and his whole gestalt feels like he could be my brother. *I love it.* I love looking at brown eyes. I don't care how he got to look the way he does. I don't care what the explanation is for why he looks like he's my brother. He looks like a Cypriot Greek or Levantine to me. We look the same. That's all that matters to me. Now... since I'm dark-skinned, or olive-skinned, there is no problem with my walking into an entirely black place with him. What those people think is that we are two light-skinned blacks.... And there's no problem with his walking into a predominantly white group with me. People think that—

That's very funny. You can both pass.

That's right.

That's hilarious. You can both pass as both.

It's a contextual thing. And I think that's what race is anyway. I mean, who's to say what we are? My mother says to me with some conviction that we have to be entirely Cypriot with no black in there because we're a family, we're generations of families, of Orthodox priests. Well, orthodoxy includes Moors and Algerians and so on and so forth. And he looks the way he does because he has a mixed ethnic background, and I don't know that mine isn't.... I can't be bothered with it. But I don't want to cause my mother any grief. Actually she responded well. I was very surprised, so I knock wood on that. She just said, "You mustn't let the relatives know." They can meet him, so on and so forth, but "just don't broadcast it." Because she's got to live in their world. She's just crossing her fingers that we don't have a dark kid. I mean, she's not a racist as far as Mark is concerned. Or as far as blacks are concerned. But she's got to live in a very parochial Greek Orthodox world. She hates it, but that's it. So I can do that for her. I mean, my Aunt so-and-so is never going to come to Chicago. And I'm never going to live in New York, most likely, unless Mark wants a transfer after his kids are grown. So there's no reason for them to know, and I will respect my mother's wishes in those regards. No, it's not an issue. It really doesn't matter.

What do you see as the major sources of conflict and danger to this relationship?

Insecurity. Jealousy, but jealousy is only a mask for insecurity. Mark is concerned about when I get out into the world and work — and this is the first time in my life since I got my working papers at fourteen that I haven't worked continuously. My parents stopped giving me money 'cause I left home when I was sixteen. So I was self-supporting at sixteen. And throughout college I've always had a job. Mark says it's okay for me to go to Jimmy's, the local student bar, because he can't think of a better place for me to go by myself. There are nothing but ugly men in there and dumb men — men that I'm never going to look at.

But he *does* feel threatened about my being in a professional association with other men. Because that's not a random selection of persons; we're doing the same damn thing. And he knows from working very hard in his life that if you've got a project, and you don't know if you're going to get it in under the wire, and it works, damn it, you want to kiss this red-necked bastard right next to you, 'cause you've worked on that thing together. Well, that's what he's worried about.

How about children?

Well, children's a big issue. I want kids, and I don't think that's negotiable. If I were twenty years old, I could think about marrying him in the hopes that he would change his mind. But I would be kidding myself to think that. Look at it this way, I have to take him at face value. He says he doesn't want kids. He already has three. He spent his twenties raising a family and not developing himself. I have real sympathy for the guy. I mean, here he's thirty-six years old, and his youngest child is ten. Why should he want to go through diapers again?

It's a situation that I really can't answer right now. My mother tells me — and I don't think it's such a friendly thing — but what she says is "Look, if you bargain away that business now, when you hit your mid-thirties, you're either going to fight about it all the time, or you're going to sneak and get pregnant." Now it's *not acceptable* that I would get pregnant without his permission. And the way we deal with that is he takes a huge responsiblity for birth control, because I say to him, you have got an unconscious and so do I, and we'd better check each other, because if I get pregnant, I am not going to have an abortion. The only way I've been able to grapple with this for here and now is: I know him, I don't know my kids yet. I know him. And maybe he'll change his mind, but I'm not counting on it. And I really don't know what's going to happen when I'm thirty-eight years old or forty and I still don't have a child. I just don't know what's going to happen.

The thing is, Mark was hurt by not having been given a vote on the number of kids or when they came, and I could never do that to him. And I have no solution to that. The only way I can cope with this possiblity that I might not have kids is to say, well I know him; I don't know them. It's going to come to a loggerhead. But if he came home with a vasectomy, I'd be shattered. I'd leave him. Because at least now, there — and I'm probably pointing out some basic contradictions — but at least now the door's not entirely closed. He could change his mind. But I'm not counting on it. Maybe if he goes back to school and if he's really happy with his life and who he is, maybe then he won't see more kids as a burden, but... anyway that's the future. Who said the future would be easy?

Sally & Beth

The Viking
on the Battlements
and the
Chicken Soup Lady

I met Sally and Beth in their two-story pragmatic house — whose foundations were at the time being massively reinforced — situated across the street from a small factory in the mixed residential and industrial hinterland of Oakland. Inside, their home is bright and comfortable, surprisingly and stylishly colonial; we sit on a rug before a roaring fireplace. Beth is in her mid-forties, with dark curly hair and fine features, animated and attractive. Her quick intelligence and desire to charm shine through her conversation. At fifty Sally is a tall, commanding New England Quaker lady — she reminds me of Katherine Hepburn at her most cracker-barrel majestic. Her conversational style is homey, shrewd, comfortable and utterly direct. Both are professionally involved in psychotherapy and members of the broad "therapeutic community" of the Bay area.

BETH

Tell me how you met Sally.

My first memory is hearing about her. That's where it began. Her son was in my group. And—

A therapeutic group?

A personal growth group, the first thing of that kind I had ever been involved with. It was a big deal for me to go there because... I lived in the suburbs, and it was in Oakland which was the city, and in a very bad section of Oakland — as a matter of fact just up the street here. I had never been in this section of Oakland before. People like me didn't go to these places.

Anyway, Sally's son Robert was in the group. He was a nice young boy, and we started to meet for a few minutes before the group and have coffee together. I guess I chose him to talk to because he was the only person in the group I felt comfortable with. Everybody else was — it's a funny story — the men had beards and long hair, and the women wore these Indian sack dresses and were barefooted, and to me everybody looked like they had BO and hadn't shaved in years. I was astonished and frightened by the whole thing. Robert at least was clean-shaven and looked familiar to me. He looked like my son who was the same age, twenty.

And I remember sitting in Dunkin' Donuts while he told me

about this woman who was his mother, and she sounded just *fantastic*. She was about the same age I was and she had four children and was studying at the University that year. Without a degree, and I'd never heard of that before. I was convinced then that I would never have a degree myself, I would never be more educated, I would never be anything much. It was *fascinating* to hear about this woman. And he talked about her *a lot*. I had an *image* of her — although I'd never laid eyes on her — and my image was a very tall attractive woman.

Were you straight at this time?

I was *very* straight. I was so straight I used to come into Oakland in a green and white polyester pants suit, with makeup and high heels, Very straight, very elegant and so forth. And I felt very uncomfortable. It took me a little while to realize it was really because my mode of dress was so different. Of course, I was different inside, too. And one day I decided I wasn't going to be uncomfortable anymore, so I went to a store and bought my first pair of jeans, an Indian top, and some beads and flat sandals. And I came to group the next week wearing this outfit, and everybody just applauded. I had made this great transformation. I tried not wearing makeup, and that was hard, but I got used to it after a while. And I felt even more comfortable then.

It was a strange group: people screamed and beat on pillows and yelled into the air at people that weren't there. It was all very strange to me.

Then one day after group somebody said, "Oh, here comes Sally." And this is my second vivid memory. She was down at the end of the block when I looked up. And that's an image I will never forget: I saw this tall, very attractive, *commanding* looking woman. She must have been wearing a cape or some crazy thing — in those days it was *all* crazy to me — and she takes very big strides so she just fills up my vision. She walked towards me, and I thought, Oh my *God*, she looks just like I imagined her. Everybody was vying for her attention. I wanted to say hello and introduce myself; I genuinely wanted to tell her what a wonderful son she had because he and I had become really good friends. But she didn't pay attention to me. She

just said, "Oh yes, isn't that nice," and "thank you," and that was
that. But I never forgot that image of her. Even when I think about it
now, I remember the feeling I had. It wasn't a feeling of sexual attraction. It was just a feeling of a very overpowering person.

I was in the process of separating from my husband by this time.
We were in couples therapy, and I wanted to go into my own private
therapy. I asked the co-leader if she would see me. She said no, that
she didn't have time but she recommended seeing somebody by the
name of Sally Standish. I said no, I wanted to see *her* because I had
built up a trust with her. But she said I'd have to call Sally.

I remember the day I called I was terrified: I sat on my bed and
dialed the number about five times before I let it ring through — only
because it was another strange person that I was going to have to tell
about myself. That was very hard for me at the time. And she didn't
remember who I was, which made it more difficult. Then she started
talking about money, which was something I didn't talk about.
What did I know about money? She told me — I'll never forget it —
she said that it would cost fifteen dollars an hour. She could have
said fifteen thousand dollars because at that time I didn't have any
money except for household money, and Sidney certainly wasn't
going to pay for it. And I didn't want to ask him to. I remember
saying yes I would pay, and having no idea where I was going to get
the money. But I committed myself.

We talked about where to meet, and *mercifully* she said I didn't
have to meet her in Oakland, that she saw clients at her commune.
When I heard *commune*, I didn't want to go there, because to me a
commune was a bad place with bad people. I hadn't known that she
lived in a commune. Then I thought, well it might be fun to see what
a commune looks like; I guess I'll try it. So I said sure.

The commune was eight minutes from my house on the free-
way. And the day I first went I was an absolute wreck. I rang the bell
and I will never forget: she came to the door and opened it with this
sweeping gesture. It was like — remember Loretta Young on
television? Well that's the way Sally opened the door. Her hair was
long — it was sort of flying. She had on huge carpenter pants and
some kind of skinny little top, with I don't know what kind of shoes
but they weren't what *I* called shoes. And I thought, good God! *This*
is the therapist? I mean I had Freud in mind. I knew she wasn't Freud

but I figured when I saw her professionally she would be dressed. And then this house! It was dirty, there weren't any carpets, the curtains were hanging cockeyed, there was junk all over — it was what I had imagined a commune would be. My worst fears. And I was scared. I really was scared.

She asked me to go up to her room — it was a combination bedroom and office and sitting room — and I remember sitting down in the chair she offered me and being so *nervous* I couldn't talk. But she put me at ease very quickly, and soon I was absolutely enthralled with her. I had never heard things like she was saying — I just had never heard about life, basically. I only knew one way of life. Also she was listening to me and validating my experience, which was the most important thing because my mother had always told me: "Don't be ridiculous. He doesn't drink, he doesn't smoke, he doesn't run around with other women. You should be happy. Look, you have a house and two cars and horses and children, etc." No one had ever said, you may have all those things and still be unhappy. Or that there were other ways to live, which had never even entered my mind.

So listening to her week after week, my *world* began to open and, as frightening as it was, there was something very supportive about Sally. Not only that she had done it — the kind of therapy we do is a very sharing kind of a situation, and she would tell me about herself, about her ex-husband, her marriage, her children, her divorce, making her mark on the world and so forth.

At what age did you get married?

Nineteen.

So you had lived at home, then got married and lived with your husband?

No, I went to college for two years. I had gone steady with Sidney when I was fifteen, and then we broke up and saw other people. I was engaged at eighteen to another boy whom my father didn't like. He just stood up to my father, and my father didn't like that and told me he didn't want me to see him anymore. It was as simple as that. And I said I wouldn't. Because I always did what my father said. As a matter of fact I always did what anybody said. Until after I was married I never did what I wanted at all and I didn't do much of that after I was married either. But that's what I was taught to do.

So Sidney and I started to date again in the summertime, and he was a very kind person. He's a very gentle man. And he's a very good man. He's a little crazy now but he wasn't then. He came from a nice family and he was headed to Cal Tech, and my father thought he was wonderful. He was very quiet and very polite. My father would say things like, "You really love him, don't you?" And because I never disagreed with my father, I would say yes. And that's how it happened: I became convinced because my father would say every so often, "You really love him don't you?" And I said, "Oh, yeah."

I was a sophomore in college when Sidney graduated and had to go into the service — he was in ROTC. He called me up one day and said he'd been assigned to Wright-Patterson Air Force Base. And I don't know how I ever said it, but I said, "You're not going without me." Which had a lot to do with the fact that at the end of two years all the girls I knew got married — that's what everybody did in those days. This was 1951. I was at a girls' school in Maryland, which was very strange in itself: being Jewish and never having left New York, my parents sent me to this woman's college in the South. I'll *never* figure out why they did that. My father thought I was safe. I was. There was nothing for me to do there. I mean *no* social life. And for me it was doubly hard because I didn't date boys that weren't Jewish, I wasn't allowed to. So I couldn't go out with any of the local boys, and the colleges around there were St. Mary's, a Catholic school, Notre Dame, and Annapolis. And there aren't any Jews in those places, so I didn't date. That's why I kept in contact with Sidney so much during that time. So at the end of two years everybody got married, and so did I. That's what happened. My father was *delighted*. He thought that was the most wonderful thing.

So we got married. Had a big wedding with all the trimmings and so forth, and I went off to Wright-Patterson Air Force Base with Sidney. I was just nineteen a month. And the only time I'd been away from home was when I went to college. Five weeks later my parents came to visit us on their way to see my sister in summer school. And I asked them to take me home. They said no, "You

made your bed, now lie in it." My mother told me it was too soon —
he was really a nice boy, and blah, blah, blah. My father said,
"You're not coming home. Doctor's daughters don't get divorced." In
those days people didn't get divorced, and certainly not doctor's
daughters — my parents were both doctors — so I didn't. In talking
about all this in therapy with Sally, I did what most clients did. I
became very attached to her. I became very dependent on her. Have
you ever had any therapy?

No.

Well, that's a phase you go through. Transference. And in gestalt
therapy that's not worked with very much, but nevertheless I certainly did experience transference. One or two times I had some
fantasies, but I knew it was transference. I was in training myself, by
this time, and I knew what I was going through. I was sort of amused
that I was doing the same thing that other people were going to do
with me at some point. It never occurred to me that I was attracted
to her in any other way. The therapy was going along fine, I was
busy separating from Sidney, going through all those trials and
tribulations. The first time Sally and I made personal contact was
one Friday afternoon when I came late. I was distraught, I don't
remember about what. She offered me a glass of wine after the
session. I didn't drink in those days, so a little wine absolutely sent
me for a loop. I couldn't see straight. Then she suggested that I call
Sidney and tell him I wasn't coming home for dinner. I had *never*
done that, in twenty-five years I had never not been there for dinner.
So I said I would. And I called him and he was as dumbstruck as I
was. I mean, looking back on it, it was really very funny: he was so
surprised he didn't even ask why. He just said, "Oh."
  Sally asked me to go to a women's bar with her that night
because she was going with her daughter. But a women's bar to me
didn't mean a gay bar. I thought it was a bar that women went to.
Number one, I never went to *any* bar. And number two, I was
curious to see what this women's bar would be like.

Why was she going to a women's bar?

She had promised her daughter that she would take her. They were
going to spend some time together.

Were either one of them gay at this time?

No, no.

So it was just. . . a mother and daughter doing an interesting thing?

Right, having dinner and then going out. And afterwards they were going to meet some other friends from the commune at another bar in Oakland. When she asked if I wanted to go, I said sure. Why not? She made dinner and she had this crazy way of cooking — I watched her put all these vegetables together in a pot — everything was different from what my mother did. But I was absolutely enthralled watching her make a meal, to see that there wasn't any concern about whether the plates matched or how the table was set or where we ate or who was there. People were wandering in and out and eating from the pots. Everything was so haphazard. My life was very structured and neat, everything happened on time and in certain ways, and this place was a *madhouse,* and I loved it. And her children obviously loved each other. Two of the girls were there at the time. My own children fought like cats and dogs — our house was very unpleasant.

So we went to this women's bar, and you have to believe that I didn't even know the people were gay when I walked in. Then I looked around and began to see that people were different, and when I realized where I was, *I just laughed.* And started to enjoy myself. Even got up and danced, though *I didn't dance.* Sidney and I hadn't danced in twenty years. But here were all these women dancing together, and I danced.

But when you realized that all the women, or a lot of the women, were gay. . . .

All of them.

It didn't frighten you? You weren't freaked out by it?

It *was wonderful.* That's what I remember thinking. I had a wonderful time. I didn't want to leave. I remember saying, "Oh, I don't want to go." And Sally was laughing. I guess I danced with Sally, but I didn't have any particular feelings about it. After that we left, because Sally's daughter was upset, she wanted to go to a straight place and get her equilibrium back. So we went to another bar. And I had some more wine so I was really pretty cockeyed by then. Sally says that in the other bar, which was very crowded, I stood behind her and put my head on her shoulder. I remember doing that, but I did it because I was falling over and she was the person in front of me. She experienced it differently. But that's where I was coming from. Really.

How did you get home? Did someone drive you?

I had left my car at Sally's house, so we went back there, and I took my car and went home. And — uhm — I never thought about it again. It was a wonderful experience, but I never thought about it again. I went about my life. I was embroiled in a divorce and I had my own problems. I kept going to therapy, but there wasn't any attraction, other than Sally was a wonderful person and my therapist. Then finally Sidney moved out, and I terminated therapy. By this time I really liked Sally a lot, but it was always a therapist-client relationship. There was never any stepping over the line as far as either of us were concerned. It never occurred to me that we could be friends, or would be friends. Number one, because I generally felt that way. Here was this wonderful woman, and why would she ever want to be friendly with me? That's how I felt. But after Sidney left the house I had this big party, and I invited all kinds of people and I thought of Sally. And I said, Gee, that would be nice. I need to know some single women; I'll call her. So I did, and she came. With her daughters. We had a good time, and she was the life of the party as usual.

When did you see her again?

She had said as she left, "Give me a call sometime when you have nothing to do, and if I'm not doing anything, we'll do something together." I remembered that because part of my therapy was trying to do things that I never did before — take risks. I would never call up a strange person and say, "What are you doing?" But I decided, Okay, she said that, I feel safe with her. I'll do something different. So one Saturday I called, but she was having dinner with a friend, and I guess she said it was a man. I said, "Oh. That's fine. I'll call you back another time." She said, "No, no. I'll see what we're doing and call you back." When I hung up I thought I would make other plans because I had never heard of a woman inviting another woman to come out to dinner with a man friend. Then Sally called back and said come. And I thought: this is weird, but I'm going to go. Why not? So I did.

Did you know this guy?

She had mentioned him.

Did you know he was her boyfriend? Or that they were sleeping together?

I think the word she used was "my man Jay." Or something like that. That meant to me that they had some connection. But it was an ambiguous kind of statement and I didn't pay much attention. I had in my mind they were a couple and I was the third person, which is why I couldn't understand why she wanted me to be there. I would never have done that. But it was a nice dinner. Jay was pleasant and easy to talk to, though I don't think I said very much. I sat there watching the two of them and looking around the strange house — she had moved out of the big commune into a small one. They didn't have any furniture, just mattresses on the floor in the living room, and a table, and a couple of old beat-up chairs. After dinner she said something about going to the bar across the street, which I really didn't want to do. It's not the kind of place I would ever have gone to. But they were going, so I went.

There was some dancing and Jay asked me to dance, which was fine, although I really stayed away from him because he was Sally's man. I thought he was very handsome, which he is, and I liked him a lot. But that was out of bounds for me. We went back to her house and sat on the floor. I remember dozing off periodically because I was really very high on wine.

I knew I had to go home. I had two children at home. I had never not gone home in my whole life. But I also knew that I couldn't drive, and I was a little scared — how was I going to get home? There was a lot of conversation, some of which I could hear and some of which I couldn't, because I kept dozing off. And the next thing I knew, Jay was gone and Ruth, Sally's housemate, was there. I remember Ruth on the floor talking to Sally while I sat to one side, on the mattresses. And I vaguely remember moving over and putting my head on Sally's shoulder. But if I did it, again, it was sort of a dropping onto somebody.

I had no idea of having any kind of relationship with her. I don't even remember Ruth leaving. But the next thing I knew Sally said something to me like, "What do you want to do now? What is this all about?" Or something. I didn't know what she was talking about... I really didn't. So I said, "I don't know." And the next thing I knew it was happening. I just... there wasn't a moment in between that I could even say I knew what was going to happen.

So you started making love?

She started. But I... agreed. Without any hesitation. And I knew somewhere along the line that I wasn't going to go home and that concerned me a lot. But obviously not enough. I worried a little bit about what I was going to tell my children the next day. But that didn't seem to worry me too much either. I remember wondering Where the hell is Jay? And what was that going to be like for Sally? But I was very drunk and I was enjoying myself. So I guess it didn't bother me enough to do anything about it. Later she said it was time to go to bed and that her daughter was away for the weekend, so I slept in her daughter's bed, and she disappeared. I fell asleep instantly.

When I woke up in the morning, I think I was the one that was not particularly in shock. I just... I was so blocked at the time, I don't think I knew what I was feeling. I really had some concern about Jay. I think I was a little embarrassed. But I didn't know whether he knew or not, so I didn't think too much about it. We had breakfast and I didn't want to go home but I knew I had to, so I did.

Had you ever made love to a woman before?

Uh-huh, 1962. When I was married. That was sort of a time out of time. That's hard for me to talk about.

Was that the first time?

Yeah. She was a friend of mine named Sandra, and I had a dream that I was making love to her. And I remember waking up in the morning and thinking, Oh my God, that's ridiculous. I wasn't particularly frightened — I just thought it was a little strange. Then one day she was sick, and I went over to visit her and she was in bed. I was sitting on the edge of the bed talking to her and she told me she'd had a dream about me. So I told her about the dream I'd had, and she just sat up and opened her arms to me, motioning me to come to her. So I did. I was surprised, I'll tell you, because it had never occurred to me before. (Laughter) And I felt... it felt really nice. I was very fond of her.

We had a relationship that was quite intense for about six months, I guess. We would see each other during the week, but we never said the word homosexual or lesbian. "Is this strange? Are you frightened?" We never talked about that. It was just something that happened that was very beautiful. Lots of fun. I remember telling her it was the best sex I ever had. When she left, I said "I don't think I'll ever have sex like this again." I don't know where that was coming from. 'Cause I had fine sex with plenty of men. But I said it.

So it was definitely a sexual relationship, you explored each other physically and all?

Yeah. And to make it sound even stranger, we never talked about it. We just did it. We just did all kinds of things I'd never even heard of.

It wasn't just cuddling?

No, we were having a sexual relationship. To me, a very bizarre sexual relationship — that's in retrospect — because she had a lot of ideas that I had never heard of. But I went along with everything and just had a wonderful time. A lot of laughing and fun and warmth and play. Like children. And very serious sex. So it was all those things rolled into one, plus a wonderful friendship, 'cause we had been friends for about two years. But we never talked about it. I never gave it a moment's thought, except how wonderful. And that was that. When she left, I was sad. And... I never thought about it again.

That's one thing I want you to believe. When I tell you I never thought about it again, I mean that. I never thought about it again. Until I was with Sally and she asked me if I'd had other sexual experiences with women. I said, "No, of course not." Then I said, "Wait a minute." And I remembered. But I had never thought about it. It never occurred to me to look for another woman. *It just didn't occur to me.* I just went about my life. Which is what I did most of the time.

How about after the first night with Sally? Were you shook up? Did it seem like a momentous event?

It seemed like a perfectly natural normal comfortable thing to do. And I was aware that my body had responded in a way that I don't ever remember responding to anybody, any human being, except maybe Sandra. That was lovely. It felt like a relief. There wasn't any pretense, I wasn't embarrassed, I wasn't scared. I was just there. I mean, when I was married, I had a lot of sexual relationships with other men, but they certainly weren't wonderful. And my husband and I had sexual problems. But it never occurred to me I was gay. I don't think I was at the time. But the feeling with Sally was, How wonderful! I couldn't wait to see her the next weekend. She had invited me to this party and all week I was in love. It was as simple as that. I was just in love. And I think I knew then that this was it. I didn't know whether she was available; it didn't *occur* to me that I would ever live with her. But I knew that I was going to be in a relationship.

The man I had been going out with, he suddenly faded. I had also been seeing three other men, and I told them during the week I didn't want to see them. And I just thought about her. Day and night. It was a tremendous emotional relief from my divorce.

It never occurred to me about getting caught. It never occurred to me about being a lesbian. I never had any of those thoughts at all. I just knew it was wonderful; she was a wonderful person who I admired and respected and whatever that kind of love was, that's what I was feeling. My whole body was alive and awake, which it hadn't been for a long time. The next weekend when I went to the party at her house, I couldn't wait to get there. But she ignored me — she was very busy being a hostess. She'd apparently been feeling scared during the week, but I didn't know that. It didn't occur to me that she'd be scared. I was just so dumb. (Laughter)

You decided after one night? That you were in love and that somehow or other you were going to be together?

It wasn't even a *big* decision that I sat down and thought about. It was just... you know how you just float? That's the way I felt. This was what it was going to be. And the next week I remembered that I had a vacation coming up from work and I didn't know what I was going to do. Why not do something with Sally? So I went and asked her if she would like to do that.

The second time you saw each other you asked her to go on a vacation?

Yeah, we had spent one night together. But the following week I said, "How about going on a vacation together?" She said she was going away with Jay, but she would see what she could do. Later she called and said that she could. *I* don't remember making love with her again until we got to Oregon, but she says we did so I guess we did. I think it was one big blur for me. We didn't go until August, and this was in July, so I'm sure we saw each other; I just don't remember. I had absolutely no interest in anybody else after that. She's the one I focused on.

The trip to Oregon started off like two women going on vacation. We went in my car, and I was very excited. I had no idea where we would go — that's right, I forgot about that. We didn't have a reservation. I never went *anywhere* without having a reservation in the finest hotel. And she had this crazy idea that we were going to go to Oregon and find a cabin in the woods. I don't know anything about cabins in the woods. Besides she wanted to live in a *crummy* cabin in the woods. I wanted to go to a very nice hotel. And she said absolutely not. She told me we would find a place to be, and I thought, Well, she must know. So I go off to Oregon with this strange woman, not having any idea where I'm going. Really. And having the utmost confidence that it was going to be just fine. And we did, of course, find a very nice place. It all materialized just the way she said it would.

I remember laughing at the time, I was absolutely delighted. All of a sudden *things* didn't seem to matter so much. I was very... what could I say... I was so focused on what was going on between the two of us that the outside world didn't exist. I forgot about my children; I forgot about my house; I forgot about everything. It was the first time in my life I had ever done that. And when she said that she had brought acid — I had *heard* of Timothy Leary and this craziness with LSD, but it had never touched my life.

What year was this?

Seventy-five. The summer of '75. So she whipped out this little black thing and she tells me, "This is LSD and we're gonna do it." And I said, "Oh, okay." I was just . . . (Laughter)

Really?

Yes. (Laughter) . . . when I think about it now. I mean I would never do that today, but at the time I just assumed she had done it before, that she knew what it was all about. I never even asked her if she had. She hadn't.

What was the acid experience like?

We got up in the morning, early, 'cause she said it took eight hours to come down. I remember sitting at the little table while she cut it in half and gave me a piece and told me to put it on my tongue. We sat there, and I remember saying to her, "Oh nothing's happening; it's not working." The cabin was paneled in knotty pine, and I remember looking up and seeing the *panels* move — the knots were sliding. I said, "Something funny is happening." I remember looking at my hands and seeing that all my fingers were sort of attached together. But I loved it.

My memory of that whole trip is a lot of fun, a lot of laughter and sitting around looking at these strange walls and the way everything was moving around. One important thing for me was that I realized that everything I thought, she *said* a split second before I did. Which is *exactly* what happens in our relationship. And it was so clear when we were under acid. I would have a thought and she would say it. It happened all day long.

I remember crying about that. I felt like somebody was taking my thoughts away. We talked a lot about that later, because that's been an issue with us. She is seconds faster than I am, sometimes more than that, but generally speaking seconds faster. So she says everything before I have a chance to. And that has made me withdraw many times.

I know we went through some terribly emotional scenes. I wrote about it, so I have it on paper. But my memory now is of feeling her as a very powerful woman who was out in front and that I was behind. Which seemed to be all right, because she was constantly assuring me that I would catch up to her. And I believed her. I remember her making me write out "I will get whatever I want," or something like that, and signing it. I dropped the pen on the floor and asked her to pick it up, and she refused. She absolutely refused to pick it up. And I remember thinking, "Oh, she's teaching me how to take responsibility for myself." And, in fact, that's what she was doing. She was showing me that she was not going to be responsible for me in this relationship. I had to learn to take care of myself.

What was the note you wrote to yourself?

I have it somewhere. It said that I am capable of getting whatever I want when I'm ready to get it. Which was a big thing for me to sign, because I was under the impression I couldn't get what I wanted. Not only that, I didn't even *know* what I wanted, really. I had the note pinned up in my room for about a year and whenever I felt that I was never going to go to school or do this or that, I used to look at it and know that I could do whatever I wanted to. But it was a while before I really believed that. So during the acid trip she was showing me that I had to take responsibility for myself. She would be there to help me, but ultimately I was going to have to do it for myself. That was important because the way I related to the person who was the other part of the couple — who always had been a man, but I still *related* the same way — was that he/she would take care of me. Sidney did. That's all I knew. And if she had done that, we would have gotten into difficulty, I'm sure.

So that's pretty much what I remember about it. I remember Sally talked a lot about what we learned. But, to tell you the truth, I wasn't really that aware of what was happening. If she hadn't told me, I don't know what I would have learned. (Laughter) The rest of the vacation was spent swimming and being together and making love.

Was making love with Sally different from sex you'd had previously?

It was different because I was relaxed. I don't know why. I mean this was a *woman*, and I don't know why I wasn't freaked out, but I wasn't. I was very relaxed. I was also very responsive. I had not been particularly responsive with a man for years and years. When I was young, I felt a tremendous passion — sexual passion — but as the years went by it got to be boring and old hat. I never felt much and I certainly never had an orgasm. But that's what you're supposed to do with a man, so I did. With Sally it was different.

In what way?

My body was responding. I physically felt sexual passion again, the kind of passion I felt as a young girl, which I hadn't felt in years. I felt like I had woken up. I remember crying one time, saying, "All the parts of my body work." They hadn't worked in years. And I'm very modest physically. Not quite so bad now but I was then, and she's this free spirit who runs around nude if you let her. I feel like sometimes I have to clothe her, otherwise she'd walk around nude all the time. (Laughter) That was very upsetting to me at first. But it was a relaxing thing for me too.

I was learning how to be comfortable with my body, which I had never been. I was always too fat or too this or too that. I was never comfortable. I learned in that week that someone could have a body that didn't look like Marilyn Monroe's and think it was just fine. And be comfortable with it. That was something new for me. It was fun to watch her feel so good about herself. 'Cause I'd never felt that way. So I *relaxed* a lot. The overwhelming feeling that I've had since I've been with Sally is a day-by-day relaxation of my mind and my body and my thoughts — like coming down from being so rigid and constricted for so much of my life.

Did you have to learn how to have sex with a woman?

I already knew. Remember I had a previous relationship. It's not that different anyway. And. . . Sally has a creative imagination, so what she doesn't know she creates. Of course, there was initial embarrassment and so forth, because there were parts of my body that as far as I was concerned were untouchable. I didn't care *who* you were. And Sally doesn't believe in that at all. So I had to get used to that.

Such as?

Can't you fill in the blanks?

I might fill them in wrong.

I never liked being approached from the rear by a man, never. I wouldn't permit it. I never even liked being touched from behind. I didn't even like the coming around from behind and putting the hands on the breasts. Anything that had to do with my backside I just couldn't stand. But she wouldn't put up with *any* of my inhibitions. That's what happened really. She just made believe they weren't there. So when I moved away or said don't touch me somewhere, she didn't pay any attention. And somehow or other it was acceptable. I don't know why. If she would put her hand on my ass and I moved away, she would say, "Oh, don't be ridiculous," and just go ahead and do whatever she wanted. It was amazing to me that I could respond to somebody touching me like that. I never had before. So it was a combination of watching her enjoy herself and enjoy me. I mean she *truly* enjoyed me. I don't think I ever experienced anybody enjoying me so much.

Also she *allowed* me — this is very important — she allowed me to do what I wanted. She didn't criticize. She thought it was fine. She knew that there were areas I would want to change, maybe even drop. But moment by moment she allowed me to be who I was. And nobody had ever done that before. My mother, my father, my husband, any man I was ever involved with. I always had to be someone different. And I was just fine the way I was. And in her allowing, I could change. Because before I was so damned stubborn — I don't like that word *stubborn* but when people didn't allow me to be what I was, I didn't do anything different. I just tenaciously hung on to what I was. I didn't change. But she *loved* me no matter what I did. No matter how I looked. I mean, I could stand on my head, and she would still have loved me. So I could say to myself, Well, I don't need to do that anymore. And that's really how I began to change.

I found that the more I was allowed to be, the more I began to experience a feeling of love deep down inside my body that I had never felt before. I don't think I had ever loved anybody. I began to experience what people call intimacy. Not sexual intimacy, but love intimacy. Loving, caring feelings. And I was *amazed* and delighted

— I just never thought I could feel those things. I didn't know what it was like to love somebody. Except my children. And that's different. With Sally I could make mistakes, and it was okay. I could say the wrong thing, and it was okay. I could be inhibited, that was okay. Whatever. I didn't have to know everything, I didn't have to be perfect. Not only in body and face, but in mind. And I can't *tell* you what that meant to me, I just can't. I don't have words to express it.

Sally took great pleasure in your body. Did you, from the beginning, take pleasure in hers?

Yes, I did, and I had never taken pleasure in anybody's body, any man's body... I never *looked* at a man's body. Ever. I always made love with my eyes closed. I never saw my husband naked because I never opened my eyes. And I never saw any other man. But I looked at Sally. And I loved what I saw. And in loving what I saw, I was more able to look at myself and start liking what I saw. There was one fear I had which I talked about a lot. I was afraid that she'd love me for my body. I said that a thousand times. I had enough people, men, loving me for my body. That's what they loved me for. I didn't have to be smart. All I had to do was be beautiful and have a nice body. But I did not want to be a sexual object. So it was very important that she love me for my brains too. Which weren't very developed at the time, but nevertheless that's what I wanted. And she constantly assured me that that was true. And... it's just recently, since I went back to school and found out myself that there's something up here other than sawdust, that I'm beginning to believe her. Up until this year I used to worry about that. Because if that were the case, I would never want to have a relationship with her or anybody else. I had enough years being loved for my body. And that wasn't even love.

So getting back to this first year....

That year is a blur. Our relationship was building, but it was also being fragmented. Sidney was constantly in the middle causing trouble: he didn't send the money, etc. You know, the usual things men do during divorces. Running around telling everybody that our marriage was bad because I was a lesbian. Now he knows. I was terrible and disgusting and all the rest of it.

Did that upset you?

Of *course* it upset me. But I soon learned that nobody paid any attention to him. All these people knew he was a little *meshuge* anyway. Nobody deserted me, so I couldn't have been so terrible. He would catch me in the garage in the morning after he had moved out. I would go out to go to work at eight o'clock, and there he was in the garage. He would corner me against the wall and scream obscenities and carry on. It was very unpleasant. And I was frightened of him. Financially. At that time I didn't know whether I could earn a living, so I had visions of being out in the street and not having any place to go. I don't know what I would have done if I hadn't known Sally. I'm sure I would have survived, but it would have been more difficult. I would probably have continued to go out with men and gotten married very quickly. For security. And because I needed an ego boost. That would have been disastrous.

But it didn't happen. And Sally was there a lot. I was more at her place than she was in my house because she didn't like it in my house. And that was one of the beginnings of — I began to see a difference right there. My home was very beautiful and very expensive, very elegant — and she didn't like it. Number one, I thought she had a hell of a nerve saying that. I mean who walks into somebody's house and says they don't like it? I never heard of such a thing. And number two, What do you mean you don't like it? The couch cost seven thousand dollars or something like that. Not quite, but you know. And the table was five hundred dollars. How could you not like it? But she didn't like it. She said it was cold and austere and not lived in, it looked like a motel and all the rest of it . . . so there was always this pull of being enthralled that somebody could say things like that and then really not liking what they were saying at all. And her language was very different from mine. She swore, which I didn't. And she was very casual about her dress. Every little thing about her was different and unusual to me, and it was all very exciting — I was in a constant state of euphoria about all this strangeness that was going on.

It was a wonderful year. We did a lot of exciting things, and I was going to school, training to be a therapist, and getting divorced. Very difficult for me, but with her support I managed to do everything I had to do. Which is not to say I couldn't do it alone, but it was certainly helpful to have somebody supporting me.

But in spite of all these crises, it was exciting.

I remember the crises, too. I remember Sidney making all kinds of scenes, I remember my children being upset, I remember... whatever happened. But my life with Sidney was always crisis-oriented. There were *always* the crises. Nothing was easy. So I was used to it. They didn't seem like such big crises to me. Sally was not used to that, so everything was terrible to her. I was used to Sidney making a lot of scenes and carrying on and screaming and yelling and running around the house and calling me names and all the rest of it. That was nothing new to me. I was used to my children being depressed and unhappy and fighting and all the rest of it. So it wasn't any different for me.

What was different was I was beginning to see that maybe they didn't have to exist. Maybe it was because of Sidney and me together that they arose. Maybe life didn't have to be this way. That was beginning to dawn on me. From listening to Sally and watching her life, which was not crisis-oriented. So the year went by, and somewhere along the line — I don't know when, it was another thing that just evolved — I knew I was going to live with Sally when my house was sold. But before that we went to Eleuthera.

What was that like?

Sally had decided we were going to take a winter vacation. Sidney and I had only taken a vacation together once in twenty-five years. I had never heard of Eleuthera, either. My idea of a vacation was going to the Hilton, not to a cabin on an island that I never heard of before. But it was really beautiful. Wonderful. While we were there we took acid again. That trip was different from the one before. What I remember more than anything else is standing under a yucca tree talking to my mother. My mother was long dead, by the way. But that's what I was doing. I also remember putting on my negligee and deciding that there was to be a wedding and that it was mine. That I remember very clearly. I remember walking down these beautiful steps in this gorgeous garden and saying, "We're having a wedding," and apparently Sally agreed.

This was a wedding of you and Sally?

That's what I decided. Sure. I'm very practical and I know that women can't be married legally — I remember thinking about that. And I wasn't a great believer in any kind of ceremony other than legal. But under the influence of acid I decided that was ridiculous and we could have a ceremony. And that I wanted to marry Sally.

So we had this little ceremony. I remember walking around and feeling like Ophelia or something and being very sunburned. And when we were coming down, Sally and I took a walk to the beach and climbed up on a dune. I remember picking up a little tiny shell and giving it to her as a wedding present, and feeling at that moment that in fact we were married and I wanted to be with her the rest of my life. And feeling a little foolish because women can't marry, and knowing that that experience, that moment, was going to be something that was only between Sally and me — nobody else would ever know about it.

Then I did something that was very out of character for me. I was wearing my daughter's terry-cloth bathrobe and I didn't have anything on underneath. And I took it off. (Laughs) I can't believe I did this. Standing on top of this dune, I took it off. I was absolutely stark naked. I just stood there, with the breeze blowing. It was like a movie, it was just magnificent. There wasn't another soul around, just this high dune with magnificent foliage overlooking the Atlantic Ocean. And just feeling warm breezes on my body. And Sally took off her robe, too. We both stood there, and I knew that I was married. I said a few things to her but I don't remember what they were. And this little tiny shell which she has on a locket was... it could have been the Hope diamond, that's how beautiful it was at that moment. And how much it meant to me to give it to her. As far as I was concerned, I was committed in a way that I never knew that word could mean. I knew that I would be with her the rest of my life. And would... I remember thinking that I would do whatever I had to do to make sure that I was with her for the rest of my life, which is something I'd never felt before. And that's how I feel now....

So then, when you came home....

When we came home—

You moved in together? Or not together?

Well, when we came home my house was on the market — this was in March '76 — and I sold the house sometime in May. I knew I was going to live with Sally. We hadn't talked about it particularly, but I knew that's what was going to happen. And it did. Her roommate was moving out, and I was going to move in.

I assumed I was moving in with my youngest daughter Valerie. The rest of the kids were out of the house by then. We fixed up a room for her, painted it, bought a carpet and so forth. But about two weeks before the move, my son came over and said he wanted to talk to me. Wanted to tell me that he and his father had been talking to Valerie; Sidney had been talking to Valerie, and had decided, *she* had decided that she didn't want to live with me. She wanted to present me with an ultimatum. He dragged her down from her bedroom where she was hiding and made her tell me that she didn't want to live with Sally and myself. She wanted me to live in an apartment with her alone. And I knew that I couldn't do that.

How old was she?

Sixteen. 'Cause I knew that if I did that, we would hate each other first of all. And second, I wanted to live with Sally. That was probably the first decision in my life I ever made for *me* — disregarding my children, which was very difficult. I don't know if I can tell you how difficult that was, because my whole life had been lived for my children and my husband. And I made this decision for me. I said no, I couldn't do that. I got into the car. I left Valerie crying on the front lawn with Warren, and I got into the car and drove off.

Sally was sitting on the front lawn of this little house pulling weeds. I got out of the car, walked across the street, sat down in the weeds, and I said to her, "I just left Valerie. I'm going to live with you without her." And I told her what happened. That was very hard for me. And also very easy. Because I knew I was doing the right thing. For me. And somewhere underneath I knew that it was probably right for Valerie, too. Because Sidney had a lot of money, and I didn't. He could keep her there where she was going to school and keep her with her friends, which he did. And let her finish her two years of high school in the town she grew up in. So it wouldn't be so disruptive. And I wasn't sure if Valerie would be comfortable living with me and Sally. I really wasn't sure. So the decision was hard, but underneath I felt that it was a good one. I knew I couldn't live in an apartment with her alone. I just knew it. So . . . .

So you and Sally moved into Sally's house.

I sold my house. Everything got straightened out. Lisa, my other daughter, went to live with her boyfriend and her brother Warren. who had a little house that he'd rented with his girlfriend. The two young couples moved in there. Valerie went to live with Sidney. And she was devastated. She was really devastated. It was a very hard time for her. I went to live with Sally and that's when all the adjustments began. And our relationship—

Who else was living in this house?

Paulette and Susie. Paulette was a friend of Sally's from her other commune. We had been friendly.

And Susie is . . . .

Sally's youngest daughter. So I moved into this little tiny house with what was left of my furniture. Because it was such a small house, I had to sell a lot of furniture. What you see here is what I moved in with. And in the space of four hours this little house became gorgeous. All the pillows and the mattresses and the rags on the windows disappeared, and my furniture was put in this house. It was a lovely little house, it just didn't have anything in it. When the draperies went up and the furniture and so forth and so on, it was transformed into a very nice house.

And I moved in with the expectation that everybody would treat my things the way I treated them. 'Cause I'd never lived with anybody else before, except my husband. I assumed I would have the same kind of respect about not only my belongings but my privacy, which I had a lot of because Sidney and I didn't communicate. And that Susie was like my children and would have the same respect and so forth for me and my belongings. But those assumptions were dashed very quickly. That's how we started to have trouble. I felt terrible most of the time. I felt nobody cared because I equated caring for my things with caring for me. Sally pointed out over and over and over again that loving a table had nothing to do with loving a person, and slowly but surely that began to sink in. That may sound simple, but it took a long time. and some of my things were hurt and broken and destroyed, which caused a lot of trouble. They just lived very differently than I did. They sat on kitchen counters and put bare feet on kitchen tables and did things which I just didn't do. And it was hard for me. But through all of this, Sally and I were very close. There was a lot of fun in the house, too; Sally has a way of making things seem not quite so important. I can be very intense about everything. I began to lighten up a little bit and not take things so seriously. Paulette was altogether spacy. She was an enigma to me. I've never figured her out. Fortunately she moved out eventually.

So you were used to a much more ordered space . . . .

Much more ordered. Much cleaner. Time was very structured. I mean, I had a family. We ate breakfast, lunch and dinner when people do that. And this was not a family as I knew it. It was not a nuclear family. It was different people living different lives at different times. Nobody did anything at the prescribed times. You ate breakfast at eight, lunch at twelve, dinner at six — that's what I knew. They didn't do that. Not only that, they didn't even sit down. Everybody ate standing up at the stove or running by taking a scoop of something or other from the pot, putting the same spoon in their mouth that they put back into the pot, which absolutely curdled my stomach. I couldn't eat for a long time. And putting fingers in cottage cheese jars and then putting the jars back in the refrigerator. I couldn't eat the cottage cheese. It was very hard. Not really washing the dishes, so when I took a dish there was food on it, and I couldn't use it. It was difficult.

How did these matters get solved?

They didn't get solved. They just sort of wore away. Well, that's not true. When Sally and I moved into this house and I made enough fuss, she began to take some care, and I also began to let go. I saw that nobody was dying of poison, number one. I know it sounds silly but I think somewhere in the back of my mind I really thought that would happen. But everybody was healthy and everybody still loved and cared about each other. This was important because when I experience any kind of trauma, I go back to being very ordered and clean and start hollering, "Please put the cover on the jar," and "Don't leave things out," and "Don't put your fingers in it," and so forth. Sally impressed upon me over and over again that they were not doing this because they didn't like me but because they didn't see that it made any difference. They didn't do it to irritate me or to tell me they didn't love me. They did it because that's the way they are. And I realized that if I was going to be a good therapist, I was going to have to learn that people have different values. Otherwise I would be a terrible therapist. If I was going to inflict my values on you, why come to me? That's not what a therapist does. So I really was forced by my training, which I was in all the time, and by living with people like this, to broaden my view of life. Either that or I couldn't exist there. My choice was to learn how to do that, and it was a conscious choice. So I put up with — that's the way it felt — an awful lot in order to learn that, in order for it to be like it is now. I don't put up with it now; it's part of life. I know that when Sally leaves something out of the refrigerator, she's not doing it to irritate me. She's really doing it because she just doesn't see or she just doesn't think about it or there's something more important to do. And she'll come back and fix it later. But before it was: If you did that to me, you were out to get me. 'Cause you didn't like me and you didn't care.

But unfortunately Susie and I did not get along very well. Which is not to say I fought with her. I didn't fight with anybody really. But I didn't talk to her a lot. I didn't know what to say. And I was irritated by her all the time, by all the little things that she didn't do. She was a young girl and she didn't quite know what to make of me either. She had never experienced somebody like me. So we didn't argue but we just didn't make a connection. That made Sally very unhappy. It was a problem between us because my children adored her and she got along very well with them. They adored her because here they had finally found another mother and this one really didn't give a damn whether they picked up their clothes or not, or whether their hair was combed, which was what I always did. Here they found this wonderful woman, they could be in her house and they didn't have to do all those things, so they relaxed and really enjoyed her. Whereas I was very uptight with Susie and she didn't enjoy me.

I didn't really understand until Susie moved out how difficult it had been for Sally. And then I felt very badly but Sally, again in her own inimitable way, said "Look, nothing is forever. She's going to come home and you're going to have another chance." That's an attitude that Sally has that I didn't have. I thought everything was forever. I learned from Sally that if you argued with me and didn't like what I said, it was that one thing that you didn't like about me, not that you hated all of me forever. It was that one little thing. Sidney and I really hated each other when we argued. We could never just take one incident as itself; it was just total dislike.

So while you were getting looser and more accepting of other people's lifestyles, did they also learn to respect your need for order and cleanliness?

No, Susie did not and Paulette did not. Sally has come to understand that and has really made an effort. I think sometimes it's superhuman because my expectations were very high. My expectations have lowered, and she has worked hard to do things that she knows I like. The only time it's an issue now is if I'm upset. When I get upset, that's what I do: I begin to pick. "Oh, you didn't put the things away, and our house is dirty. Blah, blah, blah." That's me putting my world in order. Do you know anything about obsessive compulsives? That's what I do. It's so minimal now we laugh when it happens; but at the time it was very important to me.

But what happened was my world began to be safer. I felt better about myself, I was learning skills, I was beginning to see clients and feeling good about myself. I certainly loved Sally very much, and I knew she loved me. My children's lives were coming together. Sidney had stopped yelling by this time. Everything was getting better in my world, and I was feeling more secure, so I didn't have to worry about all this structure that I had built up. So the house didn't get cleaned on Friday, so what? It wasn't so terrible. I felt safer. I didn't have to do obsessive things like that. Which left me a tremendous amount of energy to do other things. Which is what happened, of course.

Did you stop seeing Sidney altogether?

No, and there was one important incident. Somebody was sick. I don't know which girl is was. Valerie or Lisa. Anyway, he came to see her, and, to tell the truth, it never occurred to me that it would be so traumatic for Sally. Just like it doesn't occur to her to put something in the refrigerator, it didn't occur to me that it would be traumatic for her. Also, I wanted Sidney to see where I lived, although I didn't know that consciously then. We had a lovely home, and I wanted him to see that I could make it without him. Because his parting words to me were that I would never earn a nickel, and I hope you die of breast cancer, and all the rest of it. I wanted to show him that I was intact and in a good relationship, living in a nice place and earning a living and so forth. But I didn't know it would affect Sally so much.

How did she react when you told her Sidney was coming?

She went up to the bedroom and she *locked* the door. I couldn't believe it. I mean she had never locked the door on me. She totally withdrew from me, for the first time in our relationship. She was lying on the bed and wouldn't talk to me and was crying, and I didn't know what to say. I didn't know what to do. I was very torn between Sidney and the children downstairs and Sally upstairs. It was the first wrench that I felt between us. I knew he was only going to be there for a few minutes. I mean he didn't plan to stay, he understood that. And so I . . . she says, and I vaguely remember, that I told her to stay upstairs. I mean I don't think I handled it very well, but I didn't know what else to do. And she stayed upstairs, and he left. And . . . it wasn't because I didn't love her; it wasn't because I was trying to do anything to her. I simply did not have any conscious awareness that it was going to affect her that way. I didn't know a lot about her feelings of invasion, because my life was constantly invaded. I mean I had lived with invasion. Sidney was a . . . he invaded my privacy. All the time. And I was constantly surrounded by children. I didn't know what it was like to have my own private space, my own room that nobody came into unless they knocked. And it would never occur to me to tell somebody not to come into my house. So I didn't understand the feeling she had when this man who had caused so much trouble — besides being my ex-husband — came into her little house. I had no idea what that meant to her.

How did you two deal with it?

I told her I was sorry. But... I felt obstinate. I felt like I didn't know what to say and I didn't know what to do. I felt angry at her for causing this trouble. Yet there was another part of me that was saying — I remember so clearly — saying to myself, you've got to do it differently this time, Beth, because this is somebody you love and you have to pay attention to what's happening to her. I think it was one of the first times in my life that I was able to not to say to myself, "You're right and she's wrong." I was able to say, "Wait a minute, there has to be something to this. Take a look at what it is and talk to her about it." Sidney and I didn't do that. I was right and he was wrong, or he was right and I was wrong, that's all there was to it. So it was a moment in our relationship — probably the first — when I was able to look at what she was feeling and say, "There has to be something to this, I'd better take a look at it." And we made up.

Immediately? Or did it take a while?

As far as I remember, it didn't take very long. I don't think we've ever been angry with each other for long.

Did you two ever have contact with Sidney again?

Oh yes, at Valerie's graduation from high school last June.

You were all together?

Yeah. We all went to the graduation. I thought Sally and I were going to be over here — it's a big village green — and Sidney was going to be over there, and I didn't really think... I mean we might wave to each other, but I didn't have any sense that we were going to be together. I thought that would be nice, because it is our daughter, but I didn't see how it would happen.

Sally and I were sitting on a blanket, and Lisa came over and said, "What would you think about going out to dinner with Daddy and Joan?" Because Sidney has a woman friend. And I said, "Oh, no, I don't think we would do that," but then Sally said, "Why not?"

And I said, "Wait a minute, that's... let's talk about this." Because I knew how she felt about Sidney. Then Sally said, "Look, it's Valerie's graduation, and I feel secure enough with you that I want to do this." So I said to Lisa, "Go tell him it's fine."

But I want to tell you something before that. It was a very beautiful, sunny day on the village green, and everybody was in white carrying roses. The graduates were walking down, and Sidney was standing taking pictures. And I went over and stood next to him. It was an important moment because I felt like we were together at our daughter's graduation. I also realized at that moment that I was very separate from him. I mean he's the father of my children, there's a tie between us. But I knew at that moment that the tie was very different. Yes, we were the parents of these children, but I was not connected with him emotionally anymore in any other way. So that was very important for me. And I was able to tell him that.

Once that was over, we all went out to dinner and had this bizarre time. It was really funny and very emotional. I get a kick out of watching Sidney. I was able to look at him as another person, not as my husband or even ex-husband. And he does have some delightful traits. He was kind of sheepish as I was too. And we started to talk about money I guess, and Sally cut in and said, "Wait a minute, don't bring up that subject because that's always a touchy subject between you two." So we didn't, and the children and Sidney and I just had a nice conversation. Sally was busy talking to Joan and they got very friendly with each other. It was really very funny, and Sally was wonderful.

And the rift between you and Valerie?

That seems to have disappeared. She's in this house all the time and she writes me wonderful love notes and we are close. I think at some point in her life, when she's in therapy probably, she's going to have to deal with the fact that I left her. Sally keeps saying, "No, you didn't leave her; she made the choice." Nevertheless I was her mother and I chose not to be with her. I consider that leaving her. To her father whom she *did not* get along with and did not want to live with. She's gonna have to deal with that, I think. But everything is really good between us now.

So that year I was learning more and more about my career and not experiencing a lot of trouble around being in a relationship with a woman. That was not an issue for me. Every once in a while I'd look at Sally and say, Oh my god, you're a woman. And I would laugh. She would say the same to me. But that was all. We didn't do a lot of socializing: we were too busy seeing clients and going through training and workshops and things like that.

When did you decide to buy this house? Was that a big move?

Yes. We decided to buy a house when Sally's mother was sick. Her parents needed a place, and Sally wanted to bring them here. I felt that was a good thing because if it were my parents, I would have wanted to do the same thing. And I wanted to buy a house anyway because I had gotten money from the house I sold and I knew that it had to be invested again. I knew it was reasonable to own a home as opposed to rental. So I was agreeable to buying, but for me it was too fast. *Much* too fast. I mean when Sally says she's going to do something, the next day she does it. When I say I'm going to do something, it takes me three months to do it. Again that's our pacing.

We hadn't even talked about where. I hadn't lived in a city since I was seventeen; Sidney and I always lived in the country or the suburbs. So we went around and looked at some houses that weren't terribly appealing, and then the real estate agent called and said to come see this house. When I heard where it was, I didn't want to go. But Sally said, "Oh come on, let's go." So we went, but I really didn't want to come in because I knew I wouldn't like it. But I came in and I walked around grudgingly and then I walked out and said no. I wouldn't live here if you gave it to me. I really meant that. But what happened was I... Sally stopped pushing that night, and I felt guilty. Here was her mother dying, and they had to come and Sally said this house was going to be adequate, and, to tell you the truth, I hadn't even looked very hard at this house. I walked in and saw what it looked like and walked out. But Sally said it was going to be good. It was *her* parents, so I gave up. I remember feeling that: I gave up.

But I was so... I was very much in love. That was the main thing for me, that we had a good relationship. I have lived in

$100,000 houses and then in this one and I just decided that maybe it doesn't matter. So I said okay. Let's do it. And it was not a good choice for me in many ways — the first year was hard. I didn't say a lot, but Sally knew it. It's somewhat easier now because I don't look. I have a wonderful capacity for not seeing if I don't want to see something. I go around Oakland and I don't see, I just don't see. But the fumes kill me. I see the house-buying decision as coming from . . . I would do it for her parents. I would want her to do it for mine, so I did it for hers. And it had to be immediate. One thing I know is if you have to do something, you do it. So we had the house redone . . . which interestingly enough did not cause any difficulties. I mean, with such different tastes, such different styles, it was really wonderful how we worked everything out. It was fun, and we learned a lot about each other doing that.

What sort of things?

I went to all the stores and picked out all these things absolutely convinced that Sally would never agree to anything I wanted. Most of her comments about what I liked were "Yuck." That's the word she used. Eventually I had to ask her not to say that because I felt it was a put-down. So we learned to respect each other's taste and decisions. And we learned very easily. That's what's so wonderful. If she said she liked this and I said I liked that, we either said okay, or else found something that we both liked. Actually it was fun. Sometimes when I wanted what I wanted, I pushed for it. There were definite things I wanted and would not be without.

Like?

Like a garbage disposal, a dishwasher, a stove that did the things I wanted it to. There are certain things that I would not be without. And curtains on the windows right away. And she said okay.

There wasn't a lot that she insisted upon, that she couldn't live without. She would have been happy to paint and paper this house and move in the way it was. But I absolutely refused and because of that we spent a lot of money. I think it caused her . . . I *know* that it caused her some difficulty because she didn't have a lot of money to spend and, not only that, she wasn't used to spending money on those kinds of things. But if I couldn't have the comfort outside the walls of this house, if I couldn't look outside and see beauty, what was inside had to be at least acceptable to me. I had to be able to get up in the morning and look at something that was pleasant to look at. I could not live in this house the way it was. I don't care who was dying. If she didn't want to pay for it, I had the money to do it. But that didn't happen. We just split everything down the middle. Oh, we were really funny. Down to the last penny, we split evenly. Which was a very good thing.

Do you own it jointly?

Yes. Every single thing in this house is half. Everything. And that was very important because I had money and she didn't, and that easily could have become an issue. But because of her father's insurance, she did get some money. So we just kept it even, right down the line. And when we couldn't afford any more, fine. I already had most of the things I wanted anyway.

How do you feel about the house now?

I love the inside of the house, down here. I love this room. This is a haven for me. I like some of the rooms upstairs. If I had my choice, I wouldn't live in it, but it's okay. It really is okay. I'm comfortable. I wish it were airier, but that's beside the point. I *like* to come home. I like to walk into the house and know that it's mine, it's ours. When I walk in the door I feel peaceful. And I never felt that before. I used to come home and feel my insides were being torn out. And when my children come into this house, they say the same thing. That's why they love to come here.

How would you say your relationship has changed over the last four years?

One thing is I no longer feel like I'm behind. I feel like I have not only caught up to Sally intellectually and in my career and emotionally, but in some areas I feel I have surpassed her. But I don't need to surpass her anymore. I am very comfortable being where I am and when I feel like I'm a little bit behind, it's okay now.

There's no competition between you because you're both therapists?

Oh, yes, That's a very big issue. We're both very competitive women. I didn't really know that. I mean: who was I competing with, my husband? I realized in the years that I've been working that I *am* very competitive. We do co-therapy, we run groups together, and there's intense competition. It's an issue that we're still working on. But it came from my feeling of being inadequate. And I don't feel inadequate anymore. It's really fine now. We share information and share skills a lot. Yesterday, for instance, was a wonderful day, it was really just like two people bouncing off each other, working all day long in perfect harmony, which is fairly new for us. Being able to work with Sally and do it well is the most important thing for me. Loving comes first, and being able to work with her comes second, and — this is the first time I've ever said this — I think sexuality comes third.

Have there been any changes in the sexual relationship?

Yes. That's where we've had the most trouble. (Long pause) In the beginning our sex was fine. There wasn't any trouble at all.

Did you ever have — this may be an ignorant question — sex roles?

I think that's what's changed. Sally, being a more assertive person than I in the beginning, was the initiator more than I was. My role as a sexual being was always the passive woman. That didn't change just because I was with a woman. I never experienced being with Sally as being passive, I was actively available; I wasn't just lying there saying, "Okay, do me." But it's true that she initiated sex more than I did. I went along with it instantly, but she initiated it.

As time went on and I became more involved in my work, I think I took my passion and put it into my work. I have stopped being readily available sexually. I simply don't feel sexual a lot of the time. And I don't reject her, because what's happened is that she's stopped initiating. And it became a vicious cycle. When she felt that I wasn't feeling sexual — she senses every single time I *blink* my eyes; she's very attuned to me — so when she sensed that and felt that as rejection, she stopped initiating, and the more she stopped initiating, the less I felt sexual because I didn't have to rise to the occasion. And she stopped initiating more, and I stopped feeling more until we got down to almost no sex life. And the emergency bell went off, so to speak, and we ran off to therapy. Actually I think I suggested this.

Because when I first lived with Sally, I told her that if we couldn't have a good sexual relationship, then I didn't want any relationship. I lived with somebody for twenty-five fucking years without a good sexual relationship and I'm not about to do that anymore. So I said let's go to couples therapy, which we did. We learned a lot about transitions in relationships and how sometimes the sexual cycle is up and sometimes it's down and, you know, the old story. And it's not resolved. It really is not resolved. But there's a tremendous difference now from what it was in the beginning. We work very hard all day long and evenings, and I'm damn tired. And I'm not faking it either. I'm exhausted, I'm drained. I just don't have it. But when we don't connect sexually we begin to distance ourselves, just like anybody else. And Sally feels it much more acutely than I do. For me it's very important to share with her at the end of the day all the passion I've thrown into working with these people. To me that is almost sexual... I come downstairs and I'm so high and I discharge it all. Then I'm exhausted; I go to sleep. And I do know that that's cheating her — that really is cheating her and cheating myself.

I don't know what to do about it. I don't see myself stopping working very much — I am only in the third or fourth year of my career. Sally is in the seventh or eighth of hers. I'm just beginning to taste the joys of success financially and personally; I'm just beginning to develop a reputation. Until very recently I always depended on Sally for my referrals. Now I go places and somebody says, "Oh, Beth. Gee, I've heard of you." Whereas before it was, "Oh, yeah. You're with Sally." So I'm just beginning to become a member of the therapeutic community in my own right. For me this is very new, and I am not about to give it up. *But,* on the other hand, I am willing to struggle and work to do whatever we have to do, if that means going to therapy, if that means scheduling time, I'm willing to do it. But I'm not willing to give up my career. She's not asking me to, but I'm not even willing to give it up much. Which is going to cause a problem, and I know that. I mean I'm telling you this now. I don't think I've even said it to Sally.

Have other people ever been an issue?

Other women?

Yeah. Or men.

No. Time and time again women have said to me, "Beth, you're not a real lesbian." And they said it very angrily. According to whatever a real lesbian is supposed to be, I'm not it. I am not attracted to other women. I have never been attracted to another woman, other than Sandra in the sixties. But I am not attracted to men either now. So no, no problem.

Since you've been with Sally, you've had no sexual attraction toward anybody else?

No.

How about Sally?

I don't think so.

Would you feel threatened if Sally was sexually attracted to another person?

I think that would depend on when you ask me that. If I am seeing a lot of clients and very involved in my work, *"Geh mit gezundte hagen"* (to use a Yiddish expression) go with — do your thing, don't bother me. But I suppose I would be threatened. See, I know what being involved sexually with someone outside of a relationship can mean. I know perfectly well. When I was involved with other men, that was detrimental to my marriage. So I make the assumption if Sally were involved with another woman, that's going to be detrimental to our relationship, and that something is wrong with it. If I was happy with my husband, I don't think I would have been involved with other men.

But then there's another part that asks, Are human beings monogamous? Can I live for the next twenty or thirty years without being involved with another human being sexually? Is that what human beings do? I don't know; that really remains to be seen. But from past experience I know that sexual involvement with a person outside the relationship means danger. I haven't asked Sally to be monogamous. Not directly. We have talked about it, and we are in a monogamous relationship, and. . . I can't imagine what would happen.

But I don't let anybody get near me. I do not let any other

women get near me. I ward off their sexual vibes the same way I would ward off heterosexual male vibes. And I don't know whether that's because I feel that I might be vulnerable or because I'm not interested. I think it's because I'm not interested, because I'm not. I don't know what a psychologist would say. I *do* know what the psychologists would say: they would say that I was scared and that I was pushing people away. But I don't know whether I really buy that. I am not interested; that's all.

What arouses my passion with Sally is working well with her. That is sexually exciting to me. There's some kind of a connection that comes from my past. My parents were both doctors and that's what held them together. I am not my father, but I'm very much like my father. I look exactly like him. Put a moustache on me and see my father. I know that I get very passionate with my work and I can translate that into sexuality sometimes. So those are the two areas that arouse my passion, and if I don't have those I'm dried up and I could blow away. Which is what happened in my marriage. So... you asked me what has changed sexually in our relationship. The frequency of sexual contact has changed dramatically; it's much more infrequent than it was. The intensity of it when it happens is different also. Yet when there's a connection — like yesterday there was a very strong connection in our working together, and I felt very sexual. And the sexual contact this morning was very, very passionate for me. But it's less frequent than it was.

When you describe the early years of your relationship, Sally's presence seemed to so fill your imagination and make everything else peripheral. That must have changed, given that you're now so involved in your work.

That's changed... but you also have to remember that even during my working hours Sally is very present. She's right in the next room. I always know she's there. And many times when I'm with a client, I think, Oh, if only she were here!

So her presence looms as large now?

Her presence is very important to me. Remember my parents worked and lived in the same house, just as I'm doing. And I really believe that's what held their relationship together. And I think I've done the same thing. If I were here alone, I wouldn't give a shit, to tell you the truth. I would have to go out to an agency and be surrounded with other people. I would not live a life in this house and practice here all alone. Sally's presence is very important to me. If she's not here at the end of the day, I don't like it. I allow it, because she's an autonomous person and so am I. But that's the icing on the cake for me... for her to be around. Which is not to say that I could not exist without her, because I know that I could. But that's what makes life beautiful for me. I love her; I respect her. And we're colleagues and lovers and friends. And that's very important.

How... this is a difficult question... one could say that Sally led you out of Egypt and into the promised land, so to speak. In the promised land do you find you don't need her as much?

I think that is a fear of hers. And I have tried to tell her that it's not true. I know that careerwise I could carry on by mself, but I love her. And I want her. And the need for her I feel is appropriate, because in a loving relationship there is space for needing as well as wanting. Does that make sense? So there are times when I appropriately need her. And I *always* want her. But there's a difference between need and want, and I know the difference. I could be an independent career person and emotionally I could carry on independently too. But I want her. And that's very different than having this intense need for her. There were times at the beginning of our relationship when I couldn't let her out of my sight. I don't have that anymore. I know that I'm an independent woman and I also know that I need her sometimes and want her all the time.

There are some people who would say that's not good, you need to be able to enjoy your experience for yourself. I *can* enjoy an experience for myself, but it's *better* if I enjoy it with Sally. That's all. And that's the way it is. (Long pause) So the major change in our relationship is the autonomy that I feel. I'm able to go out and go to school and have a lot of good feelings about what's going on and feel very independent and separate from her and yet come home and feel very close and together. I no longer feel like I'm a burden to her. I am an independent woman and can care for myself emotionally and financially, and also want to be with her.

You wanted to talk about your intellectual differences?

Yeah... Sally is much better read than I am — she's very well read — and much more curious than I am, her mind is stretched in a way that mine is not. But I don't have to feel bad about it because I know that's happening for me, and I think about so much more now than I ever did in my adult life. I enjoy that and know I'll think about more and more as time goes on... 'cause it's *only* four years that I've been out of hiding, so to speak. I don't need to feel bad about not knowing everything right now. And that's very important because I spent a long time feeling really bad about what I was. I don't do that anymore. So that's a big difference in our relationship. Sally doesn't have that burden of me feeling bad about myself every time we go out. I've accepted a lot of responsibility for myself, almost total — financially, emotionally, intellectually. Because of that she is much more free to come and go and do what she wants to do without it affecting me the way it used to affect me. It's no longer a child/parent relationship. I really feel like we're two peers, and that feels very good. And that's also true sexually.

What do you mean?

When I want to have sex with Sally, I will ask, and if she wants it, she will ask. I don't necessarily worry about rejection anymore. Uh... I don't know what she's going to say about this, but I don't have a lot of concern about our sexual relationship anymore. I know it's going to ebb and flow but I think it's going to be all right. There was a time when I worried about it a lot.

Was there ever a time when you worried about or doubted whether Sally loved you?

(Pause) No.

So you've always—

I was so egotistical! (Laughter) It never occurred to me that she wouldn't! My big fear was that she wouldn't love me intellectually — she would only love my body. But once I realized that wasn't true I just believed her because it's more than words that she says; it's her whole way of being with me that lets me know that she loves me, and I'm not afraid. I think the one way I could destroy that is not to connect with her. If I distance myself and I get so involved in my work that I don't need her on an emotional level, that's the way I could push her away.

But Sally's very upfront with her emotional needs?

Absolutely upfront. She says what she needs and what she wants. Otherwise I could drift away and I wouldn't know that I was drifting. For twenty-five years I lived like that. But we've been living together for three years, and that's not a long time compared to twenty-five years of living with somebody else. So I'm learning all the time, and so is she. I see this as a long-term, loving relationship... which means forever as far as I'm concerned.

I'm convinced that everything is going to be all right because it is, and it has been, and I don't even feel any qualms about saying that it will be... because my commitment that day in Eleuthera was so deep nothing's going to shake it, and if there is something, I don't know about it. We have such a beautiful thing together that I don't see any reason why it shouldn't happen — not at all. I really don't. I never said that before.

SALLY

Tell me how you met Beth.

I should give you a tape Beth made as a Valentine present for me — the story of our meeting. She did it as a fairy tale, and it's very nice. But it made me a little confused about her view of how we met and my view of how we met. My view is that I was not prepared to deal with her very closely. By then I had learned to defend against too many people intruding in my space, since I was working with so many people at the Center....

As a therapist?

As a therapist and group leader. So when Beth came up to me and said, "Hello, it's so nice to have your son in my group" and "Such a dear," I just handled it lightly without really engaging with her. And when she called me saying she wanted a therapist to help her get out of her marriage, I was reluctant to take her on, so I insisted on my fee and I tried to ship her off on some other people. I didn't feel good about making that connection for some reason, but she wasn't about to be put off. So I saw her and I liked working with her. She was easy to work with.

Had your son ever said anything to you about Beth?

After she approached me I said something to him, and he said,

"Yeah, she's neat." But that's all. Anyway, working with her was a pleasure. She's a good student, she'll take risks: she did some heavy work in our four months together. She separated from her husband in the course of those four months and had some pretty heavy times. She was filled with bad feelings. There were moments she felt suicidal, and once she called me up from a bar saying she didn't know if she could get home — she was too drunk. I told her she had to get home, and that was part of growing up. I certainly wouldn't go down and rescue her. She wanted to be protected. I held my boundaries, even then.

So then she worked through a separation from Sidney and decided she was ready to try to go out on her own. She lived in her house with her two girls, and ummm... one evening we went out together. Now this is — I'm embarrassed to tell this story because I feel so naive, it looks like such a setup. My daughter Linda was visiting, and this one Friday night Beth came for her appointment at about five in the afternoon. I was going to take Lindy out for the evening on the town. As a matter of fact, I guess I already knew that I was going to show her a women's bar. I had been there once before, and it was exciting because there were all these women and all this women's energy and I had danced and it had been a wonderful experience to just feel that free. And I told Lindy that I would like to show her that and would like to see if she felt the same way I did.

This is basically a lesbian bar?

Yeah. But as far as I knew, that was not the big hit for me. It was the sensuality, the dancing, the women's energy. So at the end of the session Beth was saying she didn't want to go home and I said, "Well I'm going out with Lindy tonight; if you'd like to join us, you're welcome." So she stayed and had dinner with us in our little commune. There were the three of us... no, Susie was there too. Beth was really very impressed with the way we operated together as a threesome. It was the first time she had seen something that was not a dichotomy between children and parents. You know, she said: children are children and parents are parents, but that isn't the way we behaved at all. And Lindy and she and I went out to this bar, but it was completely different that evening. It was full of butch type people, sitting around tables. We sat in a booth, and there was me with my beautiful daughter. Lindy was getting all these looks and was freaking out. She was really getting scared and wanted to get the hell out of there, but Beth was turned on, she was having a marvelous time, it was her first experience in a bar. There I sat between my client and my daughter and I didn't know what the hell to do, so I said, "Lindy, hang on. We'll just dance once and then leave." So after a dance or so I said, "I'm sorry Beth, we've really got to go." It was hard to get her to see the importance of taking Lindy out of there. But we finally did, and Lindy said she needed a hit of a regular kind of bar, so we went up here to Tom's, which is an integrated heterosexual bar. Beth was high — she was in that energy place — it's a sexual energy, there's no doubt about it — and I mean she really had a lot of energy, and when I was standing with Lindy watching the dancers at Tom's, Beth was behind me, and she put her head on the back of my shoulder. And... I felt I had broken the bounds of the client/therapist relationship. "My God, she's turning on to me! Oh dear!" Literally, that was my reaction. I mean, I was just simply horrified. So I left Lindy there and said I had to go home.

I remember walking down the street with Beth, to her car: I was walking on the ouside of all the parking meters; she was on the inside. And I was doing it as a game, but I was conscious that I needed to make space between us. When we finally got home, I sent her on her way and resolved not to be social with any client until we had worked out that therapeutic relationship.

Had you ever had any lesbian experience before this?

The only experience I had was one evening with a couple of friends of mine. I had asked if I could stay at their house so I could get to work the next day without going all the way back home. I didn't know they had a friend living with them. At dinner all four of us sat around a tight table, and I literally felt like I was being seduced. They started talking about orgies and more than one or two people in sex relations and drinking a lot of wine, and, whew! I was getting very turned on to the whole idea.... I remember clearly going and taking a shower because I knew that this was it. Then we all sat around the living room, and nothing happened... I was sort of disappointed.

But then the couple went off to bed, and the woman and I were in adjoining rooms, separated by a large archway, on two open-out couches. And I got up and I said, "Listen, you know I started getting turned on by all that talk and I want to tell you that I'm still in that place and I would like to know if I could come over to your bed" — so I was the aggressor at that point. She said, "Oh well, all right." I went over to her couch, and I was just sitting down when I hear patter patter patter patter, and down the hall comes this couple, and they got up on the bed, so that was a very nice experience.... He was irrelevant to me, but I really did enjoy the women. I was very happy with that. And that was my only experience.

That didn't lead you to think you were a lesbian?

No, it was just an experience. I'm trying to remember when that was in relation to Beth. I think it was the summer before.... A couple of years before that I had felt an attraction to a woman who had seduced me — not sexually but just as far as my feelings were concerned. She was in my group, and I realized that I was attracted to her and I thought to myself, My God! I could be attracted to women. And it turned out that she had already done exactly the same thing to all leaders in whose groups she had been, including the men. Nevertheless, the feeling had been there, and I talked a lot about it with my colleagues and explored it. And one night one of my colleagues had a party, and I was high and silly, and I'm very physical, rough-housing and physical, and she said to me, "Don't put the make on me." And I froze! I went underground for a couple of years. My one recognition of the possibilities of that thing was smashed. So this thing with the three other people was the first time I had let any of that out.

After that evening with Beth you resolved not to see her again?

Not to see her socially at all. And I kept very cool. When my daughters and I went out to her party — it was at the end of therapy and even then I remember being very much in my role that day, very conscious — I heard her talking to her ex-husband on the phone, getting sucked in, and I stayed distant from it, not becoming a friend at that point either. Even the night she called up and said What are you doing and I said, Well, Jay was here but why didn't she come for dinner — even then I just didn't realize what it was about. I think I wanted to play around, but I did not see myself literally moving over into sexual lesbianism. I didn't see myself having a permanent relationship with a woman. I saw myself opening up to many sexual possibilities but I didn't put it into the context of a switch — a permanent switch. I guess I was ducking and avoiding. Too scared.

What about this evening with Jay?

I knew I wanted her to come because I put it to Jay in a way that made it hard for him to refuse.

Jay and you were having a love affair at the time?

For seven years.

Although you lived in another city?

Yes. We saw each other about once every six weeks. We had known each other for years, when each of us was still married we'd known each other. I had called him when I was a single lady and said, "Hey, you're alone; I'm alone. Why don't we get together and find out, you know, and we can be friends." He wasn't ready then, but later we connected pretty hard, pretty solidly.

Just before he came into my life, I had decided to go to Germany to work for Berlitz, so we had three intense months when he moved into my house and lived with me. I went to Germany, and he stayed in my house, and he came over to Germany once. But we always just missed each other: he was in love with me when I wasn't in love with him, and vice versa. It just never was meant to be, and yet we have always had a loving feeling about each other, and he's been very loyal.

Anyway, Jay and I were having dinner. He liked to see me alone — he didn't like other people around. He liked to come up and play husband and wife for a weekend. He was happiest coming up and being the father to my kids and being alone with me, without any of the responsibility. Anyway he didn't really want to be with Beth but he went along with it. And in the course of the evening, drinking and eating together, the sexual vibes were flowing, and I clearly must have had them in my mind long ahead of that. In the safety of Jay's presence I really felt my own and I felt hers. And across the street was a funny old funky community bar, and we went over there and danced — each of us taking turns dancing with Jay. I remember dancing with him and saying, "This is it. This is the night of the orgy, baby. We've always wanted to have an orgy with other people; well, here you have it." And he said, "Uh-oh." And I said, "Oh, blub, blub, yourself, you've always wanted it, now relax and enjoy it." And he danced with her, but when we came back, he chickened out. He disappeared up to bed. He told me later that he was standing upstairs reconsidering, almost coming down again, and then he chickened out and went to bed. Then my roommate, Ruth, came home and she tried to "save" me for a while but she saw that was not getting her anywhere and she went to bed too. There we were, Beth and I, together at four in the morning, and I must say once I had made my mind up, I was certainly at least as much the aggressor as she was. Her aggression was more subtle. Mine was, "Okay, here we are — now what? Come on, this is where we've gotten to be, so let's go ahead." And we did. And then she went up to my daughter's room and slept the rest of the night. I went to my room where Jay was and got in bed. I had said to her on the way up, "This is a little heavy for my friend; I don't think I'll tell him all of this." And I got into the bed and I felt very loving toward him — it's really interesting, I flopped down and put my head on his chest. He hardly even woke up, but he did turn over and say, "Oh, my God, you reek of her perfume." And I knew it was all over. I couldn't lie to him the next day or not tell him, so I did. He was a little freaked by it. Beth went home very early in the morning.

What was your reaction? To physically making love?

I know I *must* have enjoyed it — I did enjoy it — but during the next week I would be driving along and I would shudder at the primordialness of it or something. I can't separate it out from what was laid on me — the societal reaction to what a no-no this is, what was after all a physical perversion. It didn't last long; the week after that I was back at it again. But there was a real time lapse.

So the first week you were freaked out?

Absolutely. I didn't go near her the next week. I didn't call her; I didn't do anything. The following Saturday she came to a party at my house that I had asked her to a long time before — a kind of nice, safe environment to have her enter as a friend. This party was fine; it was an open, picnicky kind of thing. So she came, and I did exactly as I would have done had that night not happened. She was only one of the people there, and I was being hostess and I kept moving around, not focused on her at all.

She called me up Monday and said, "What the heck was that about — you know? Where am I, why are you doing these things?" And I'm going, "I... well, I... I mean... mumble mumble." But I made another date to see her.

The next time we saw each other we were alone. I can't even remember the next date. I don't remember if we spent a lot of time talking or we just ended up starting to make love or what. I can't place it, I really can't. I know she came to my house, in the beginning, all the time, and then we went to her house, and she never stayed over all night, anytime. I think we spent a lot of time in bed. Our intellectual connection was not too great.

Then Beth invited you to go on vacation with her?

Yes, that's right. She comes strolling in the house — now, this time I guess we'd been sleeping together a couple of weeks. And she walks in and says, Let's take a vacation together — she just focused in on me and that's part of what got me — she comes marching in and says "I want to take a vacation with you." Very seriously. And I said, "Well, okay."

Which is somewhat amazing considering you'd only known each other for two weeks and that you'd never been with a woman before.

That's right, and I had a vacation set up with Jay for ten days. I said fine, I'll cut it down to five days with Jay and take five with you. So we planned to do it. And, actually, that's what I guess was so amazing: we acted out of character all the way around the whole thing. She, with her obsessive/compulsivity, didn't object to the fact that I said, "Let's just get in the car and drive to Oregon. Nothing organized." And I, for some reason, knowing she had that tendency, still didn't panic. We got to Oregon and we had to search a little to find a cabin that was right, in a place that was decent, but I never got too scared — I mean it was about five o'clock before we checked into someplace, and I don't know why I didn't panic about that. But I just had faith that we were going to find something. And it worked. We found this little cabin. And that night, oh boy, it was like there was something in the buildup of finding the cabin so that by the time we found the place we really let ourselves go — more than we had in all the time we'd been together.

So I have the memory of that being the place I was to go for broke. We had a little drinkey, gin as I remember, to let down my barriers or something, I don't know how much that played a part. It didn't become a necessary thing, but I must say there was a lot of drinking that first year and a lot of parties. How much the drinking was required for me to get relaxed, I'm not sure. And then the next day or so we took acid.

You had decided to bring acid up with you?

Yeah, I said, "I'm bringing this along." And she said, "Oh, wow, oh goodness." And I said, "Yes, goodness, we'll see if we want to do it." It wasn't as if we were planning to do it necessarily.

You had had the acid for some time?

Oh, yeah, a year or two. I had gotten some and kept it thinking I'd like to try it some time. I had never had it. If I had even once, I could see doing it. But the nerve of both of us turning on, never having experienced this drug, blows my mind. Anyway, at the time it seemed like the perfect thing to do, and it really *was* the perfect thing to do. I mean it was hysterical, it was a marvelous experience, it was funnier than a crutch, it was more passionate and deeply felt than I'd been for a long time. And I really did clearly see the problem of how we could trip ourselves up. I mean it was *clear* to me. It was like there I was, a therapist overviewing a couple and the troubles that were going to happen to these two people.

And they were?

What were they? They were Beth's powerfulness that she hid, her unwillingness to look at how much control she had in a situation. The story of her life, you know. Her not wanting to take responsibility for her control. And saying: I don't know, it just happened. So that I would be, (1) in charge or responsible somehow to hold her up and (2) blamed when things didn't go right, because I would be in charge, the initiator so much of the time. And I didn't like the way it looked and I had this absolutely clear vision of me in my little Viking hat on the battlements, knocking down the Don Quixote enemies, and Beth down there with a huge pot of chicken soup stirring it and helping the wounded and mixing with the crowds. And it was just such a clear picture.

And she said, sometime in the course of this trip, "It'll happen as long as I want it to." And I grabbed hold of that. I had brought everything — in case we took acid, I had brought things I thought would be interesting to have. So I had paper and Magic Markers and I got them out. I remember trying to get that damned paper opened and to get the Magic Marker and I wrote, "It'll happen as long as I want it to happen." Then I said, "Sign it because when this damn thing is over I want to have us remember that you said that, because that's key for our relationship. *Key.* That you take responsibility and you know you have the power to make things happen or not happen."

She wouldn't sign it. "No, no." It was just an amazing drama, in this little tiny cabin. I said, "Sign it or we won't have a relationship." And she said, "Oh, I can't," and she bent over and her stomach started hurting her, and I went into the bedroom, though there was nothing but a curtain. I pulled the curtain across and I stood behind it and I wouldn't come out. And she was moaning and groaning in the kitchen. She had the Magic Marker and she *dropped* it on the floor and had to pick it up, and I wouldn't come out till she signed her name on it. I still have that someplace. That was one of the big dramas. And then we'd go right into hysteria. There was a bathroom door that just kept opening and there was a sign on it, something about please don't put any Kleenex in the toilet, and it just got to be funnier and funnier, as the door kept opening and intruding in our trip.

Hours later, somewhere like three in the afternoon, we decided we had to get out and we were absolutely sure we looked obvious. We were paranoid as hell about going out of the cabin and being respectable. I got into my super dignity place, put on clothes and dressed, because we had been lying about in our nightgowns. So we went out, and there was this family right next door sitting with their backs to us who had heard us all day long. God knows *what* they were imagining. I don't know why they didn't go tell the manager to check it out: "There's something terrible going on in that cabin." (Laughter) And we came out and said, "Oh what a beautiful evening, hellooooo!" We made them turn around and say hello to us and then we marched off to take a walk. Of course, halfway down the lane we broke up laughing, we weren't really down yet. Our stomachs, our bodies were starting to have reactions coming down, so I was very uncomfortable physically.

We met a little boy who was fishing, and he talked to us, and we walked holding hands — that was a wonderful trip, not only the acid trip but the whole five days. A lot happened to unite us. Funny things, like going to the coast and coming back on a highway and forgetting what exit we had to get off to get back to our cabin, and stopping the car and getting out a map and neither of us having glasses with us and it was dark and all we had was the light from the car, and we could not read the map and we broke up because here we were — we had this vision of ourselves: they'd find the corpses next to the side of the road and they'd say, They could never find their way home. We just couldn't seem to get off that damn highway. A lot of good connections like that were made in the course of that week. And then we drove home, and she dropped me at the door, and Jay met me, and I went off with Jay.

Did you tell Jay you'd spent five days with Beth?

Yeah, he knew what I was doing. He was very upset. It was amazing how well he held up in that time. I think he still didn't believe it was real, so he was still all right. It was later in the fall — the weekend I made him confront Beth and acknowledge that we were a team and that we still wanted him to — I didn't want to lose him, I wanted him to make friends with her, and I wanted him to be in my life and — it was a very heavy thing to do to him. Two weekends we had like that. And before he left, he just sat and cried about the loss he was feeling. We had never had it, but he still felt he was losing it, you know, whatever it was.

Did you have any problems switching sexuality, as it were?

No.

You could go from five days with a woman to five days with a man?

Oh, Jay and I didn't have much sex. We went away with our three daughters. My two and his daughter. And we slept in the same room, but we had sex only one night. Going off with two teenagers who are out to meet men and one young kid is very heavy duty. And I knew one day there that I didn't want to be there. I wanted to be with Beth, and I sent him away. I sat in the middle of a field and said, "Look, you go off with the kids, I'll be along soon. I need to be alone for a while." And I wrote her a love letter and said, "Where I'm at isn't where I am — I'm with you, and this is where it's going to be, and that's it." Mailed it out.

When did you become convinced you wanted to be with Beth for good?

I think during that five days in Oregon. I didn't say it then, but I think that's when I became convinced, and it was clear when I was with Jay two days later that that's what I wanted.

So you came back from your vacation and what happened?

Beth and I just resumed. Let's see, Beth's kids had already been told by their father that Beth was a lesbian. While I was away with Jay, my housemate Ruth wrote a letter to the two of us, which I still have, talking about the wonderfulness of our energy and beauty and, you know, basically saying that we were a couple. She gave me a copy and she sent a copy to Beth, and Sidney took that out of the mailbox, we now believe, and opened it and made a copy. Based on that, he told their kids she was a lesbian and very quickly thereafter he said, It's like your mother's re-married, that virtually she was married already. So he understood that she was gone, and that didn't help much; that made him crazy. So we were careful around her kids. My kids, on the other hand — Susie was living with me — she was perfectly comfortable with it, so she didn't mind so much.

How old was Susie?

Seventeen. It was a hard year for me, both that year and the year after when Beth moved in, because I was not ready. Susie was still a young girl, she was still in the house when Beth and I first got together. And I didn't feel she was ready to be dismissed yet. I had a different attitude about the ones who had already emerged from the family, but Susie was still very much home. She was still in high school and I didn't feel like dumping her, although I had so much of my energy focused on Beth. There were lots of times when Beth would come over on a Sunday and our other housemate would be out and there would only be Susie, Beth, and me, and it was very hard for me to go in my bedroom with Beth and shut the door and leave Susie on the other side of that door. It never ever occurred to Beth. I also wanted to be with Beth, so I was really torn.

I feel that it was a lonely year for Susie. I don't think she knew that — she might now, but I don't think she did then — "You're your own person, Mama; I'm my own person." She started bringing young men home that year, and I'm not so sure there isn't a connection there. I'd wake up in the morning to find some jerk in the house, as far as I was concerned, and I had to go through that one too. "My God! My baby!" She's bringing home these little twerps, and I didn't know what diseases they had and I was still very much in my motherhood stuff, and then when Beth moved in, it was terrible. We communicated so differently as mother and daughter than Beth did with her kids. Beth was used to doing everything and yelling at her kids for not doing anything.

I was used to having cooperation. I had raised my kids in a commune since I was divorced. When I came back from Germany, Susie and Lindy and I lived alone in an apartment one year, and it almost killed us — we hated it. And we built a commune with another woman and her son so that the five of us had learned to be cooperative and live in a totally different lifestyle than Beth was used to. And they all pulled their weight, so.... But we weren't meticulous housekeepers... so Susie's way of pulling her weight was to join a food co-op and do the work involved so she could bring home all these good, wonderful vegetables and stuff at a bargain price. And one day she came in, having worked all morning — she had gotten up at the crack of dawn — and brought all this food in wooden crates and put it on that goddamned table down there — which was a distressed table, it has been in Beth's family for years and they carved initials on it and everything else — so Susie came in proudly with her gift to the house, put it on the table, and then pushed it over to make room for the next box she was bringing in and in the process scratched the wood. Beth went, "Eeeehhh" and blew away all of Susie's accomplishment. I was horrified. And I was, of course, loyal to Susie. I said, "For Christ sake, give the kid a break." We had lots of little things like that. Susie finally left. We had bought this house in April and moved in June. Between April and June the place was in total chaos, but Susie moved in here and lived as long as she possibly could, until she couldn't stand anymore and then moved out with a friend and never lived with me again. I was very sorry about the way it ended. And there's a piece of me that holds it over Beth's head.

This coming week is very important to me because for the first time all my girls are going to be here with this new Beth who understands a lot more now, and I want her to make the kind of friendship with my kids that I've made with hers. If she fails or fucks up, I'm going to be really mad because I have worked so damn hard to make a decent relationship with her kids, and I've sat with them so much that I really want her available to my kids in that way. I don't want any crap about "her things." I really want it to be different. I think she's prepared to do that now, but it was terrible then, it was not easy for me at all, it really put a blemish on a beautiful love affair.

Well, let's go back to the first year. She was still living out in the suburbs. That time, February or March, was when you took your second vacation?

Yes, that's right. February. Beth and I went to Eleuthera and brought acid — I brought the same stuff. We got it out, very carefully — this was not blotter acid, this was those black specks like half the size of Sen-Sen — and we carefully unwrapped it on the kitchen counter, and just then the one window we had forgotten sent in a gust of air that blew the damn stuff on the floor. This was a linoleum floor with black specks, so there were two grown-up ladies crawling on their hands and knees picking up specks on the floor. And we couldn't find one, we were missing one. Then somehow I put my finger down and picked up this black speck off our floor. So we got all our acid back and we took it.

But the whole experience was a very mixed one for me. It wasn't the same wonderful connection that we had on the first trip. I spent a lot of time alone, which is typical. I spent hours sitting on the sidewalk between ants here and the moon and the sun up there — they were both out that day and I was so intrigued with the macro-micro thing I was seeing. For me, personally, it was an amazing trip because I saw a milkweed plant and I watched a hummingbird come to it and get milk and then the bees come to it and get milk and I watched the milk come pulsating up through that stem, reload, in a sense, as the insects left it. So it was a very interesting trip but it wasn't the same kind of connection.... It's funny, though: she's a very funny lady when she lets down and relaxes.

Later we got in the car and drove down to the beach — I guess we had on bathing suits and bathing coats over them or something — and we climbed up to the top of the dune and there was the ocean. And Beth was into *me*, as she says; I was into *us* and history and the women behind us clear back as far as I could see — and I literally could see those women across that ocean, going back to deep in the heart of Russia and deep in the heart of Scandinavia. Oh, my God, I was into my big Viking place, and she was into her I-groove-on-you-and-now-we're-married place. I don't remember what we said, but I think we exchanged, you know, This is it, now we're married for life. And we gave each other something. I have in my locket a tiny shell she gave me. And then we went swimming. I took off all my clothes and went in the water, and we were frolicking around. So anyway... we were married and knew that we would live together the following year. And we did. There was no doubt about it. I think what's so amazing is that we didn't hesitate to do any of this stuff. We didn't hesitate; we just did things. We knew we were going to live together — so we did.

She moved into your commune?

Yes. There was Deborah, Ruth, my daughter, and me. Ruth moved out first, Deborah stayed a little while — crossed with Beth for about two weeks, I guess. Then she moved out, and we took in a new person whom Beth thought was going to be another obsessive/compulsive to balance Susie and me. And she was, until she got into our house, and then she started growing and changing and she never picked up a vacuum cleaner again for a year. So Beth lost. She felt very alone in that house for a long time, and I know it was hard on her, but it was hard on me too.

Sometimes I think she doesn't realize how hard it was on me. Jesus, I was going through changes. It was the last year of my motherhood, and it was being fucked up. It wasn't ending — sending Susie into the world — the way I wanted it to. I was compromising all over the place. And I was very hurt and upset when Susie left. She said, "I can't live with this lady anymore, I've got to get the hell out of here, she's driving me crazy." She moved over to a friend's and basically within another month she was gone. In June Susie moved to Massachusetts and never came home again. So I didn't feel like that was a very good send-off.

When Beth moved in with you, Valerie—

Valerie, her youngest daughter, was supposed to come too. That was the plan. We fixed up this wonderful attic room, painted it together, we bought her a beautiful red rug which is now in the back room. She was all psyched to do it. Then one day I was sitting out waiting for Beth to come, picking weeds in the front lawn of this little house. Beth was due to move in in a week or so with Valerie, and Beth arrived and sat down on the wall with me and proceeded to tell me this horrendous story that had just happened: Warren, with his arm around Valerie and the two older girls being more on Beth's side, calling Warren an asshole basically, and Warren calling his mother every damn rotten name in the book and saying Valerie shouldn't have to live in this terrible environment. And Valerie made her choice not to come. And I sat there weeding, hearing this — didn't let it in — and Beth was saying "I made my decision: I want to be here; I chose you over my daughter." So in a way we repeated with her daughter what had happened with mine. We made choices for each other over our youngest children.

Oh, there was one event after that. When we moved into the house, Val stayed with her father, and I came home one day to find Beth on the kitchen floor, out cold, with a knife in her hand. These are some of the little dramas I went through that year with this crazy family I got involved with. I thought she was dead. I almost died right on the spot.

I woke her up, and she was foggier than hell. And finally I got the story: she had gotten a phone call from her lawyer, saying that he had been on the phone with Sidney's lawyer, and Valerie had been there and he overheard Val saying that she'd testify against her mother and fuck her, she had no right to do the things she was doing. And Beth heard this on the phone. She went crazy, I guess. She doesn't remember anything about it. She had this kitchen knife in her hand and she passed out. I mean, I don't know what the hell she did, she didn't stab herself, but I could've killed her. I didn't know what to do, you know?

Could've killed Valerie?

Could've killed *Beth*. I said, "If you had done that, I'd have kicked your corpse. Jesus, we're the big team, what the hell are you doing, threatening yourself, threatening our relationship like that?" I mean, I was terrifed and angry.

So these little events went on happening, as Sidney kept the pace up, escalating the situation until the divorce. Beth moved in with me on June 11 and got her divorce on June 24, and then Sidney calmed down because the money had been settled. That was the big issue: How much money she was gonna get from him.

Once that was through, things got a little easier, but then the following year we had to deal with the trauma of Sidney and Valerie. She'd come up against him, and he was going through all his rage, and they'd fight, and she'd leave and come to our house, and I'd say, "Stay, you gotta stay now," and she would stay for four or five days and then go back because that's where all her friends were, she was in school there. And Beth was not inviting her back; I was inviting her to stay. Beth was... Beth held her grudge longer than I did. She said she had her chance, too late now, she can't stay here. She never told Val quite that directly, but she also never really invited her to stay. She said: You can work out the problem with your father and go back, Valerie, that's the way it is.

Then we had the trauma of Lisa. See, these kids were so used to crisis living that they picked people to live with that were crises, and

Lisa was with a psychotic boyfriend. One night Beth and I were awakened by Lisa sobbing ourside our bedroom window. I looked out, and she was half carrying this six-foot-four-inch guy through the door. I went down, and he was absolutely out of it, sitting there saying, "Lisa, honey, you're my sweet little thing." Spacey as hell. She said he had tried to kill them driving the car a hundred miles an hour and she was hysterical, and my hands got so cold I thought they were going to drop off. Really freezing. Chilled.

Beth came down, and her way of dealing with this kind of thing was rage, anger. She was furious at Lisa, furious at everybody... and I said, "Lisa, we're going to call his family, this is too big for us and his family has to be involved and we're going to get them involved." And Lisa said, "Nohhh." But I said, "Too bad, we're going to do it." I took charge. I called the parents and said, "Get your ass over here and get your son." Then I called the police, because the kid is very strong and I didn't know how he was going to react. I said I would like them to be parked in the parking lot in case when his father came, something went on, I'd feel safe with the police over there....

I mean, these little nightmares were going on all the time. That was another way I spent those three years. Heavy. Sometimes I really wonder what kept me in. I think what kept me in was some connection that was just bigger than this plane. That's the only thing I can think. I can't blame it on sex. I don't know what all the connec tions are. I think... we were so intense those first couple of years. There was sexual intensity and all this relational passion going on among everybody in that family and my connection with each one of them.

Once, I found them all out there vacuuming and cleaning the house after a very traumatic night when this same psychotic guy tried to rape Valerie and then had a royal tantrum and started pushing Lisa around, and Beth got in the middle and Beth got tossed around. And Lisa ran and fell down the stairs — I mean, a terrible night. They called me at six-thirty in the morning and I told them I'd come out at nine-thirty, I wasn't going to get out of bed and rush there, because I have a great world-saver quality and I didn't want to play into that, knowing that I have to not play rescuer to Beth's victim because I didn't buy the victim. But then to go out and find these crazy people cleaning and sweeping in different corners of the house is insane!

So we had a lot of intensity going on in those years. And when I say that life is boring now, it's that we've eliminated most of the crises — now and then Sidney hits the roof but the only one he's got control of is Valerie. She's still in his power to some degree, but basically that's been removed from us now, somewhat. We don't have to get up that kind of intensity. Now Beth takes her intensity into her work and in her development of herself. In her discovering her brain and finding she can talk to people — lecture to people — she's discovered so much in herself.

It's been a hard year for me in some ways because I'm no longer the super mentor. She's finding other mentors in the world, and I'm just the person she lives with now. That's important, but it isn't the same as being the end all and be all, which is what I was for the first two or three years. So, it's not only losing having her around me physically, to have her in touch with me physically, but also to see her finding other people who impress her more than I impress her now, with wisdom about the field we're in together. It's been a hard year. And I can get intense when she takes me for granted. Then I can get into my passion place.

Where we've had trouble is when she turns away from me — like she used to do with Sidney. Sometimes I really identify with that man. Sometimes I say, "Oh, Sidney, I know what you suffered through," and I'm not going to play the same game. Like when I get itchy and irritated about something, she escalates it and gets madder; therefore, if I want to stay mad, I have to get madder. And that's what she and Sidney used to do until they had a donnybrook. And I won't play that game. I screamed at her. "You stop taking my mad away; I'm mad, goddamn it. You can't be mad right now — it's my turn. You get mad all the time. This is mine: shut up. Just let me be mad." And often she has just moved over and gone to sleep and left me dealing with my vulnerability about her not being present for me. And we really had to hash that stuff through. So, the worm finally turned, and I became needier than she, for a change, in the relationship.

And now that I'm terribly uptight and vulnerable about the kids coming — scared to death of how they'll fit into this house and how she'll let them be in this house — I need her to be connected with me, and until a week ago she wasn't. Luckily last weekend we went to a yoga retreat, and Beth got open. She really saw me, took her casts off and saw me again. I was feeling very unseen, very itchy.

Go back for a minute, when you were first living together. Do you think the source of the conflict was cultural between you? Cultural or personal?

Cultural. And different defenses. I'm oceanic. Like it's very hard for me to finish a project down to the last detail. I leave loose ends. I almost can't box myself in, by getting it complete. Also the way I handle strain and stress is hysterically. I need to take action right away, and if I can't, I get crazy. So I call up the district attorney and create all these terrible scenes. So I'm the oceanic and the hysteric. With the WASP approach that says: I am in charge, and you are all my servants, and I can fix anything and I can make anything better, and there's always enough.

Beth is totally the opposite. Beth's coming from an obsessive/compulsive temperament, so that any time there's anything frightening, if she can just make order out of whatever in her life there is to make order out of — like vacuuming when there's chaos in her house is the way she solves a problem. Focusing down to the littlest detail, with blinders, so that she is very territorial — opposite my oceanic — hugely territorial. If she's upset with a situation, she can focus on the fact that the table is getting scratched. And then there's the cultural thing, the Russian Jewish background, which is: there's never enough, it's all going to be taken away from you anyway, nobody'll take care of you if you don't take care of yourself, everybody out there is the enemy and only family counts. It's just totally opposite mine.

But it's character traits as well as cultural traits, I think, and these opposites attract too. Certainly my oceanic "there is enough," "you'll be a therapist next year, you don't have to wait five years," that was attractive to her; and her "this is a home and this is a family and it has to be a well-knit place" is very attractive to me because I have been a gypsy for the last eight years, since my divorce. I left my house — I've never had a house since then. So the fact that Beth was a homemaker was very attractive to me. I like the fact that she stood there and said to Jay, "You know, Jay, I'm going to live with this woman." Oh, wow, I felt really taken care of. So those things are positive and negative and differences.

Do you find it different living with a woman than with a man?

Oh, yeah. It's half the hassle. Sure, we have differences, but — all right, I'll use my friend Jay because he is a white, middle-class, heterosexual man in this culture. He's sensitive, he can hear me, we can talk about what's bothering us and what we need, and then he'll fuck it up — after an intense afternoon if we decide to go out to dinner, he'll say, "Now put on makeup and look great because I'm taking you out." He needs to show the men out there what he's got. He even told me one day, he likes me to look *smashing* because he knows when he gets me home, I'm going to be all his. I don't have to go through that crap with Beth. She'll say, "Listen, look nice. I don't want to go out with you wearing tennis shoes when you're dressed." That has a whole different quality from the objectifying that a man does.

Is the sex different? Obviously it's different, but I'm wondering if it's different in essential ways between two women?

Yeah, I think it is. Now I have had some wonderful connected times with Jay, sexually it's been good. And I had a lot of good sex with my ex-husband, but I am either playing out a little bit, sado-maso, or I'm living in my own fantasies and he's got his fantasies and we're making it together. With Beth, in good sex times, it's like a blend — an amazing blend — there's a bar that's gone and there's a flow that happens that feels circular, totally circular. I think Jay and I have had that maybe once, when we had a lot of pot. But all in all, I feel like there's something to this *sameness* about bodies, you know, and the way I already connect with her, what I bring into the sexuality is freedom from the different.

Do you think physical sex between women in a passionate situation is as important or less important than between men and women?

I have — I'll tell you — power and sex and anger are so tied up, I don't begin to understand all the connections. Whenever our relationship has been threatened, we ended up making what I would have to call sado-maso love all night, and it had to do with anger, it had to do with reasserting our power over each other. I really want her to know, goddamn it, I'm here, you're not going to let go of me, baby — and that's the attitude I bring to it.

Nothing has changed since the original thesis I got on that acid trip: the Viking on the battlements and Beth by the soup. She does the masochistic thing by the soup, which is: Take me, take me, because if you're so focused on me, I have you. It's still power for her too: she's got a whole kind of power in her masochism. And that's really the roles we assume, and it's all the same stuff, it's all power, it's all, "You're mine and you're going to know you're mine and you're going to see that I'm here and you can't leave me." All entwined together. But I want us to be equals. I'm not really caught by the power thing. I *need* to know that she'll own her own power and that we're here together. If I can't keep some equality with us — that's why I won't get into any roles.

I drive the car more than she does, but boy, New Year's Eve she laid one out on me about I'm a lousy driver, lousiest driver in the world, lousiest driver she knows. I was so damn stunned, and angry anyway that I drive all the damn time. And then she can put me in the role of the dopey male — you know, the husband who doesn't give her any power, and she has to sit next to him forever and not drive. And I wouldn't drive for a long time after that. So sometimes it gets out of hand like that, but I'm watching always to not slip into roles.

My friend Jay has a very clear picture of us: he sees Beth's power underneath there and he feels that I am the one playing out the more maso role. I mean the picture most people would have is I'm the male and Beth's the female. And that makes me very angry because it's such bull. Beth's got so much energy it's unbelievable, but she plays the femme better than I do, you know. And it's true that I come on strong, but I'm very vulnerable to her. Very vulnerable. And when I get most hurt and angry is when she buys the general view of the relationship, doesn't see me in my vulnerability. Then that really hurts.

I wanted to ask you about one incident, when Sidney came to visit when Lisa was sick?

Lisa was visiting from school. She was here for the weekend and she was sick and she — there was no reason for Sidney to come into this house. Now Beth's saying, "Well, it was a power trip on my part; I wanted Sidney to see what I had." And so she was punishing Sidney and ignoring my needs completely. That's just the way I felt — goddamn it! I couldn't believe it. I felt so violated by that experience, with all we had gone through. I mean the nightmares I had been through with that woman the year before — like finding her on the kitchen floor with a knife in her hands... or coming to me at the end of the day saying Sidney had followed her around her house the whole day. And my saying, Why the fuck didn't you leave, what are you doing playing those games with Sidney? Frightening. Because I didn't know where Sidney's head was.

I mean all kinds of tales, threatening my existence because my existence by then was so bound up with her — there was such a lot of unsafety regarding Sidney: the fact that he opened her mail, the fact that she had to burn my letters. He was such a fucking violator of our privacy. But there was no doubt in my mind that once we were in our own house, Sidney would have no more power over me. And when he used to call the house at eleven at night — before she moved in he would call sometimes to catch her, you know — and want to talk to her at all hours. And I would get on the phone and say, "Sidney, this is my phone, and I do not receive calls here after eleven." "Well, then, why don't you send her home instead of keeping her in your bed." And I'd just hang up the phone, that's all I could do.

But when she moved in with me, then *we* established a home, he did not have any more power over her, as I saw it, or over me. I needed to know that. So for her to let him stroll into our house — without any warning, without any preparation, when I'm happily enjoying a Sunday afternoon and listening to music! I probably would have stayed up on my bed all day anyway. But there I was trapped in my room, with that man invading my house downstairs. I just couldn't believe it. I mean, it was Beth, in a clear sense, getting just what she wanted. I couldn't believe how cold she was when she came up to tell me. And I said, "You're what? Well then I'm coming down." I was so furious.

And she said, "Don't you dare come down if you're going to make a scene." So I didn't go down; I locked my door and I spent the day sobbing and I was really — I just felt like the bottom had been taken right out of me. It took her a long time to understand what that was about.

How did you deal with that? I mean, did you deal with it immediately, or...?

I couldn't. I was too much of a wreck. I shut my door and used up a box of Kleenex. I just wailed. I didn't give a shit who heard me, although I didn't do it while he was in the house, because I wouldn't give him that one.

She was outside the door being angry at me for not letting her in. And I was saying, "Fuck you, baby, no way." And then she just left. She just went away and stayed away until I chose to come out. I don't remember how we resolved that. I told her how I felt about it. I think I always get in trouble with her where family is all — what happens sometimes is I feel on the outside of that circle. Beth goes Clump: sister, kids, nieces maybe, and that's it. And I feel outside. And that is a very vulnerable place for for me to be.

It's like she thinks when push comes to shove, a goy is a Nazi. And that's me, you know, and now it's coming out in my family because my family consists of a German lady who's visiting soon, and Beth's telling her kids a Nazi is going to be in the house. So I get freaked by her very small circle. Most of the time I am in it. But if push came to shove, I feel like I'd be out. Not me pushing her out. If push came to shove and a pogrom started, I'd be right in the middle of it walking down the street with Beth, I don't doubt that for a minute. But I'm not sure if it worked the other way, she'd be there with me. I'm not sure. I think so, but sometimes I'm not sure.

So that closed family system is very difficult for me sometimes. It's so fucking tight. Like Beth will drop classes, she'll drop anything to be with her kids if she feels it's important. She won't do that for me very much. I'd have to be pretty laid out for her to give up stuff.

Do you think buying this house together was—

Another thing we did, like the acid trip. What a nerve we had buying a house together! When we bought this house, we didn't believe there were going to be two things we'd agree on. We thought we were going to fight our way right through redecorating and renovating. The truth is, it was a snap. I picked all the wallpaper within ten minutes, and all she needed to do was take another half an hour to look at *other* wallpaper before she agreed to it. Our pacing is very different. It freaked her out that I picked the wallpaper in ten minutes, so she took longer even though she liked it. But — we didn't have any trouble at all. We thought we would have trouble — and yet we went right ahead and bought the damn place and proceeded to renovate with a whole lot of fears, but we still did it — it's amazing.

Yes, that's quite remarkable.

I think she did believe a lot of what I said. She didn't tell me, but she did. She fought me all the way on almost everything. But I think she really did believe what I said. I think I was her way out into the world and she did decide: "This is the woman that's going to get me out into the world."

But her natural, internal <u>no</u> was operating all the time. She was against everything — that stubborn, obstinate streak she has that won't go along with anything right away. Somehow she went along with it anyway, fussing all the way. I really can't explain our relationship on any rational level. It has a depth that goes at its own pace no matter what we say and do — all my fussing about I don't want to get into this intimate relationship, you know, I have to go slowly, blah, blah. Shit, I was committed for months, but I didn't let myself say that to myself till many months after. When we started talking about moving into a house together, I think that's when I finally let myself feel that I was committed.

How do you think it's changed since Beth is in the world, today — not a housewife anymore?

I wanted that more than anything. That's what I knew she had to have for us to survive. Plus I would not want to live with someone who stopped growing. So three-quarters of me wants that, the other part has to be assured that she's not going to outgrow me — decide she's outgrown me, begin to write me off, begin to close her circle without me in it. There's always Beth's ability to tighten up, close down, that frightens me, because I don't know where I'll be. I'll either be on the inside smothering or on the outside crying. I can't stand the closing up too tight, no matter where I am.

Although here you live in the same house, work together, are in the same profession; does that feel smothering?

I give myself the illusion that I have a lot of autonomy. The truth is I don't do much. It's been months since I've made dates with women friends and gone downtown and had lunch. It's almost like I have to remember to push myself out and be more autonomous — I can't blame it on her. I need to make the space and do those things. I like doing gigs with other people. I'm not so dedicated to the idea that we should be a working team forever. That's her mother and father trip. I can easily let her do groups with other people. I have a very big loner part, very big, and the loner part competes with the insecure needy part a lot. But my loner part has to have its daily quota, or it starts feeling crushed. And I'm satisfied being in my backroom alone for the whole day. I just have to remember to get myself out of there and into the world sometimes.

Do you find that the fact that you're working so closely together makes you feel competitive with each other, and do you think that's a threat?

It's very competitive, and I see her competitiveness much clearer than I see mine, I must say. In our peer supervision group, I would say: "I'd love to talk about the structure of family therapy — I'm learning about it; I'd like to share it with the people in the room." And she'd want to make it clear that she was also learning family therapy and didn't want me to deliver a family therapy lecture as if she didn't know anything about it. Now, the fact that I wanted to talk about the structure of family therapy is probably my own competitiveness, and I'm not clear on how I do that competitive stuff.

Another place where we're hugely competitive is entertaining. We're getting much better about that now, but we used to trip over each other in the kitchen, all the time. One night we had a dinner party for Jay and another friend of mine and a couple of other people. It was disastrous: I wanted to do it the way I wanted to do it; she was upset because I wasn't putting out the right silver. There are ways to do it, and I wasn't doing it the right way. Now I *know* how to put together a dinner party with the right dishes and the silver and the whole thing — I did it for my whole married life. It's like my mother — my mother used to say to me, "Sally, I don't like living in the slums," and it was always a dig at me. Well, my husband and I were very casual people, we didn't live elegantly. But when I had a dinner party I could put it together. I had watched my mother do it. I *choose* not to a lot. I *choose* to live where I feel the moment is. If I feel that there's an elegance required, I'll put it out.

But also I've now begun to see — Beth has something that I really like, that's kind of a Japanese sense of setting. An aesthetic thing of what *feels* right: it just bothers her to see a glass salt shaker on the table when she's got her crystal out. And I appreciate her eye and, in a sense, I'm giving her credit for her taste where before I used to see it as how to please the neighbors.

What about sex? How has the sex changed in four years?

It happens a lot less. I almost feel like the classical executive: we're getting more and more into work. We escalated our hours so that we're working sometimes till eight-thirty or nine at night — and we've lost the sex drive. It went underground, and I'm still not clear whether we are depriving ourselves of each other because of some non-connection or whether we've just put all that passion into this new work, getting this house together, getting our counseling associates together, doing groups, doing our individual stuff, doing training. And we like it — I get very high, and she does too, at the end of the day, sharing the day. That's something really *good* between us.

Sometimes I don't know whether we're avoiding sex or we're judging ourselves harshly because we're not having it — as if our marr-... our relationship mustn't be any good if we're not having sex. I really don't know. When I feel distance from her and I feel her very alienated and isolated from me, I can't make real contact with her, which to me is very physical. I don't know that it's sexual but it's usually physical. I'm a very kinesthetic person, and if I don't have a lot of body touching, I get very freaked out. I feel unloved.

I don't have a handle on it. This intensity of hers is such a mixed blessing for me. I love it when it's focused on me. I love it when we're thinking together. But I hate it sometimes. She can lie in bed and be telling me about her day, and I like to stroke her while she's talking. If I'm talking about my day, I can *lean* into the strokes, or she can be stroking my body and I can still tell her about my day. But she can't do two things at once. It *annoys* her if I'm touching her when she is telling me about something. She gets annoyed at me, and I get instantly crushed and I want to take my hand away. And she's not paying attention to me, so she's not noticing my reactions. Pretty soon I start withdrawing like crazy. And then we get into a bad place because physical contact is primary for me. Not in the course of a day where she'll come up and give me a hug, that's not what I mean. I need real skin-to-skin contact, she doesn't.

Her strokes — I almost have the sense that she knows I need it, so she strokes me. She's not enjoying it the way I enjoy touching her body — I really get into it. And that is sexual. For me. I'm not sure how sexual that is for Beth. I don't need to follow through, it often feels like work to follow through and make it sexual.

When I don't have contact with her, then I blame her for not having sex. I say, "Your fucked-up family background has wrecked you because you spent years not having sex with Sidney." And I have this vision that I'm next. Jesus. Why did I think things were going to be different just because I'm a woman? She's great the first three years, and now she's turning off and she'll never turn on again.

We haven't solved that problem. When she's tuned in to me, it's marvelous: she's funny, she's seeing me, and I can be silly . . . and she laughs and she's volunteering to make contact, and it's all very marvelous. But when she's not tuned in to me, nothing can happen right. I feel always disapproved of. I feel her irritation all the time. She's focused on one, two, or ten things she doesn't have the solution to yet, and she's very irritable. She walks around looking irritable. Funnies go right across and don't register. We lose connection then, and I don't know how that works.

You don't ever withdraw or are absent for her?

Yes, but I do that in a very different way. I need alone time and I just say, "I gotta be at my desk — I've got so much to do." And I'll go up to my room and become totally engrossed in something and not see her if she walks through. I don't say, "Hi": I'm like a lump. I don't show any interest in following her around and seeing what she's up to. She says she gets very jealous of my desk sometimes.

If the sex is becoming less, at least temporarily, has the issue of sexual interest in anyone else ever arisen?

I don't think our passion is in sex. I don't think we've turned off each other, I think we simply aren't into sex. And I don't know where I put my passion.

You know, in the sixties I was a big Quaker world saver: I was out on every cause there was. I have stacks of letters to the editors I've written. I used to make sermons in churches. My passion was *up!* I was ignoring my rotten marriage, but boy I sure had the passion out there for the world.

I feel like I'm in some very contained place with that passion right now. It went for survival. Because in the last ten years I have had more education than I had all my life. I left my marriage. I didn't have a career; I didn't have a degree. I didn't have a home. I had dependent children. I had a husband who didn't support me or them, emotionally or financially. I was a gypsy; I had nothing. I've spent the last ten years getting my shit together. I don't think I've had time to think about broader issues. And only since Beth have I focused it sexually. I don't know how sexually passionate I am, but I know Beth and I have a lot of passion. I know we can turn it into sexual passion, though I don't see us being predominately focused on that.

Have you ever doubted that Beth loved you?

Oh sure, when she gets into one of those turning off spaces. Sometimes I'm afraid I'll dry out before she'll remember I'm here. And I get scared then.

Have you ever doubted that you love Beth?

No, I don't think I've ever doubted that I love her. I think there are times I don't like her, when I feel like shaking her to make her come back to me and be the woman I know she is and that I love. But I'm very constant. I was a monogamist during my whole marriage — only the last year did I sleep with somebody else, and it was in direct reaction to my husband sleeping with our babysitter. I'm constant; I'm here. I'm a Taurus, you know — I'm not going anywhere. I could really spend the rest of my life hugging Beth and thinking she was as delicious at seventy as she is now. I see no reason why this shouldn't be wonderful till we're seventy.

AFTERWORD
Passion and Decency

The six people in this book are all engaged in a fairly astonishing attempt to reinvent love outside the traditional categories, and to reinvent it in ways that actually work in their day-to-day lives. Like most of us today they experience love as a problem, something that generates perplexities and difficulties.

This is a startling state of affairs. The traditional social conventions of love, passion, and comitment don't seem "natural" anymore, they don't just carry us along automatically. It's not that they don't attract us; they just don't seem all that workable in our immediate lives. Many signs — the rise in the divorce rate, the fact that less than a quarter of all American families fit the traditional image (working father, mother in the home, and their two children), the emergence of the women's and gay movement — point to an enormous shift in our lives that increasingly renders our inherited cultural models less relevant. We are confronted willy-nilly with the formidable task of reinventing our lives, searching out and declaring our own standards, starting from scratch. Even those who uphold the validity of the most traditional forms of love and family are engaged in this process of self-creation — after all, in a totally traditional society one didn't have to assert and defend these values; they seemed self-evident and nothing else occurred to people. Today a conventional marriage is as wildly experimental as anything you can think of.

Before I started this project I was particularly interested in the questions of love and passion in the newly emerging gay male culture, not only becuase it was most immediately relevant to my own life, but because in that context these matters seemed raised with a decided freshness due to the absence of pre-existing social conventions. However, the more I talk with people, the more it seems to me we're all in the same boat. Like the pilgrims who set sail for a new world and landed on the shores of an "unstoried wilderness," we also must clear a space and build a life relying only on our wits and whatever spiritual resources have survived the journey.

It seems to me worth noting that of all the values our culture has cherished and relied upon to dignify, make sense of, and regulate our lives, the only one that retains broad and concrete vitality today is romantic love. The dignity of work, the satisfactions of the family, the nobility of the professions, the public-spiritedness of patriotism and sense of community — no doubt these values are still alive and effective to some degree in our society, but within the perspective of our immediate and particular lives, they do not seem to inspire us and provide the meaning they formerly promised. Few people today find that their work makes them content with their lives; and while we don't understand what has gone so drastically wrong with the family, most people agree that the contemporary reality falls far short of the Currier and Ives image we still cherish, but do not experience. But romantic love or passion offers all of us one of the few opportunities — outside of war — to experience an intensified feeling of reality, "just like the movies," where life makes sense and is beautiful. And everybody, from Mildred Pierce to Marcel Proust, wants their life to make sense and be beautiful.

Passionate love gives us the chance to experience the dramatic in our own lives; as the story unfolds we feel that something is at stake, something matters. In passion *who we are* matters; we matter precisely as this particular individual we are, not as worker, mother, consumer, or any other role we might play. All the great folktales and parables about love are about discovery and awakening — Cinderella, Sleeping Beauty, the Enchanted Prince. I think every businessman and housewife, every secretary, engineer, and student, goes around most days feeling in disguise — enchanted by daily routines that make us all toads — waiting for the lover who will truly recognize who we are and thereby release us to ourselves. That particular individuality our society values so highly but doesn't seem to know what to do with finds its place in passionate love; there it flourishes, an oasis in the aridity of the modern world. Popular culture is suffused with this theme precisely because it is one of the great possiblities of contemporary life.

All the people in this book experienced the intense value of passion, the inexplicable way it strikes and its nearly overwhelming power, which leaves one grasping for inadequate explanations like "chemistry." We may not understand passion but it hits with such an immediacy and certainty that while it's happening we have no doubt that it's the most important thing in our lives. As something that overcomes us, that we suffer (*pathein*, to suffer), it is not something we choose. Passion is something that *happens* to us. It is flush with sexuality, that part of us still in the realm of nature with all its arbitrary, inexplicable, exuberant energy.

Instead of condemning the increased importance we've been assigning to sexuality, our cultural commentators might consider that in a time when humanity is overrunning and domesticating the entire earth, sexual passion may be the last wild place available to us. But this final "touch of nature" still packs a wallop that can knock you on your ear. It's the overwhelming power of the experience that intensifies our sense of reality and generates an exuberant thrill — all radiating from and focused on the beloved. For it is always this particular individual who startles us and awakens the lover, the person "obsessed by a unique image which become the absolute sign, equivalent, and definition of his deepest self" (Harold Rosenberg). It is the power of desire to transform the concrete into an ideal which makes passion so important. To condemn sexual desire and passion is to try to block one of the main avenues to human fulfillment and happiness. Passion releases the magic of the concrete, it allows the earth to sing again, magnificently, as on the first day.

None of this is new, of course, but at a time when the so-called helping professions are all bent on making us "healthy" — they would have our souls walk in sensible shoes — it's worth repeating.

People have always realized the value of passion, which is why it's a universal theme of the human imagination. But whereas the traditional celebrations tend to be lyrical tragedies, stories of doomed lovers whose experience was transcendent but destructive or oppressive to the individual, what seems to me new and noteworthy today is the insistence that passion fuse with a decency that respects the person.

Since I had not anticipated this theme, it took me some time to realize I was being repeatedly knocked over the head with it, in interview after interview. "Common human decency" was something all of these people demanded and expected to find in their most passionate loves.

As I reflected on what I heard, it seemed to me that decency has two components — taking responsibility for oneself and letting the other person be different from you. Taking responsibility for oneself means not acting like a child — not, for instance, demanding the other person read your mind: "I'm unhappy but I'm not going to tell you, if you loved me, you'd know." The common mistake of trying to give yourself away totally to the other person is a falling back to the child within each of us; it doesn't work because the lover is not mother.

Straight men seem particularly apt to make this mistake when they enter a joint living situation and suddenly expect to be picked up after and served — probably because life with mother is their dominant experience of living with a woman — but anyone can make the same emotional mistake. Some part of each of us wants to give ourselves away and return to the emotional security of the child, who knows that he can ultimately leave responsibility for everything to his parents.

It's easy to make this mistake because passionate love does seem to be a total acceptance and affirmation of one's being, which is the great and necessary emotional experience of childhood. But in an adult, trying to give oneself away is a mistake. It is a misuse of the opportunity that love — that spectacular confirmation of our existence — offers us, which is precisely to release us to be ourselves, "in a world which is doing its best, night and day, to make you everybody else." (e.e. cummings). Besides, it doesn't work.

The other side of taking responsibility for yourself is not assuming you have to take responsibility for the other, letting the other person be who he or she is, a person quite distinct from oneself. This fact sooner or later emerges when the early haze of passionate bewitchment begins to burn off. It seems to me this reality leads to disillusion only for those who make their experience of love so self-centered that it leads to a structural paranoia.

The fact that you are hurt does not necessarily mean someone set out to hurt you; not every action of the lover is taken in immediate reference to the beloved — a fact that is oddly clear to us about our own actions, but not about those of our lover. I know that a passing disinclination to sex or a preoccupation or need to be alone does not necessarily mean I am no longer in love; why is it so hard to see that the same is true about my lover? If decency in general means learning to let other people be themselves, it is even more called for in love which arises as unmitigated delight that this particular one exists.

It is hard to take responsibility for oneself and it is hard to allow other people to be different, perhaps even to rejoice in that difference. But these are the social demands of adulthood, the requirements of being a decent person. To combine this decency with passion results in a love that is very far from an adolescent fantasy, something, in fact, that adolescents are ill-equipped for. Decent passion would require that one be an adult. Love is a matter for grown-ups; for many of us, perhaps, our failed attempts at it are precisely the area in which we do grow up.

The fusion of passion and decency is what all the people in this book are striving for. It is an extraordinary demand. But it seems clear to me now that it is what I am demanding of my own life and what everyone I know is looking for. On reflection, it seems a worthwhile goal.